MOUNTAIN
BIKE
TAHOE

Previous page: *Topping out at the junction with the Tahoe Rim Trail at Star Lake* **Above:** *With panoramic lake views, it's no wonder the Flume Trail is the most iconic ride in Lake Tahoe.* (Oscar Havens) **Below:** *Rounding one of the banked turns on Jackass Ridge*

Above: *Rolling down a steep slab of California slickrock, the most recognizable feature on the Armstrong Connector* **Below:** *Taking in the view from the Tahoe Rim Trail below Mount Watson*

Above: *The top of Mount Baldy is an amazing spot to take a break and enjoy one of the Tahoe Rim Trail's best views.* **Below:** *The Clear Creek Trail in the Carson Valley is a great option when snow lingers in the higher elevations.*

Riding the Tahoe Rim Trail through the distinctive large granite boulders and decomposing granite soil of Tahoe's east shore (Heather Benson)

Above: *Flying by charred tree trunks on Tahoe Mountain's north side with a view of the lake* (Jon Rockwood) **Below:** *Blasting around a bend high on the Tahoe Rim Trail en route to Mr. Toad's Wild Ride*

Above: *Passing through fifty shades of green on the Tahoe Rim Trail on the way to Glass Mountain* **Bottom:** *The aspen trees in Page Meadows are a colorful feast for the eyes in fall.*

MOUNTAIN
BIKE
TAHOE

50 SELECT
SINGLETRACK
ROUTES

JEREMY BENSON

MOUNTAINEERS
BOOKS

To everyone responsible for making mountain biking in the
Lake Tahoe region as amazing as it is today, and in loving
memory of those who no longer share these trails with us.

Mountaineers Books is the publishing division of
The Mountaineers, an organization founded in 1906
and dedicated to the exploration, preservation, and
enjoyment of outdoor and wilderness areas.

**MOUNTAINEERS
BOOKS**

1001 SW Klickitat Way, Suite 201, Seattle, WA 98134
800.553.4453, www.mountaineersbooks.org

Printed in the United States of America
Distributed in the United Kingdom by Cordee, www.cordee.co.uk
First edition, 2017

Copyeditor: Janet Kimball
Design and layout: Jen Grable
Cartographer: Pease Press
Cover photograph: *Riding Mount Baldy on the Tahoe Rim Trail* (Heather Benson)
Frontispiece: *Popping over some rocks while riding the Tahoe Rim Trail over Painted Rock*
(Heather Benson)
All photographs by the author unless noted otherwise.

The background maps for this book were produced using the online map viewer CalTopo.
For more information, visit caltopo.com.

Library of Congress Cataloging-in-Publication Data is available on file.

Mountaineers Books titles may be purchased for corporate, educational, or other promo-
tional sales, and our authors are available for a wide range of events. For information on
special discounts or booking an author, contact our customer service at 800-553-4453 or
mbooks@mountaineersbooks.org.

ISBN (paperback): 978-1-59485-988-5
ISBN (ebook): 978-1-59485-989-2

MIX
Paper from
responsible sources
FSC® C005010
FSC
www.fsc.org

CONTENTS

Routes at a Glance **6**
Acknowledgments **9**
Welcome to Lake Tahoe **11**
Ride Locator Map **22**
How to Use This Guide **23**

NORTH LAKE TAHOE (TAHOE CITY TO KINGS BEACH)   31

1.	Page Meadows	31
2.	Scott Peak	35
3.	Stanford Rock	39
4.	Glass Mountain	43
5.	Antone Meadows and Whoop-de-doo	47
6.	Painted Rock	51
7.	Watson Lake	55
8.	Missing Link	59
9.	Mount Watson	62
10.	OTB (Over the Bars)	67
11.	Brockway Summit to Tahoe City	71
12.	Squaw Valley Downhill	76
13.	Mount Baldy	78
14.	Kings Beach Trails	82

EAST SHORE (INCLINE VILLAGE TO STATELINE)   87

15.	Tyrolean Downhill	87
16.	Mount Rose to Chimney Beach	91
17.	Marlette Peak	95
18.	Flume Trail	100
19.	The Bench	104
20.	Sierra Canyon	108

SOUTH LAKE TAHOE (KINGSBURY GRADE TO LUTHER PASS)   115

21.	Monument Pass	116
22.	Cold Creek to Star Lake	120
23.	Freel Pass	124
24.	Van Sickle Trail	128
25.	Mr. Toad's Wild Ride	131
26.	Big Meadow to Kingsbury South	135
27.	Powerline Trail	139
28.	Corral Trails	142
29.	Christmas Valley	145
30.	Gun Mount Trail	149
31.	Tahoe Mountain	152
32.	General Creek	156

TRUCKEE   161

33.	Jackass Ridge	162
34.	Hole in the Ground	164
35.	Donner Lake Rim Trail	168
36.	Euer Valley	172
37.	Prosser Hill	175
38.	Emigrant Trail	178
39.	Lloyds Loop	181
40.	Sawtooth Ridge	184

DOWNIEVILLE AND GRAEAGLE   189

41.	Downieville	189
42.	Mills Peak	195

SIERRA NEVADA FOOTHILLS   201

43.	Scotts Flat Trail	202
44.	Pioneer Trail	204
45.	Foresthill Divide	207
46.	Sly Park and Jenkinson Lake	211
47.	Fleming Meadow	213

48. Peavine Peak: Keystone Canyon to Bacon Strip 218
49. Kings Canyon to Ash Canyon 222
50. Clear Creek Trail 225

Appendix: Bike Parks **229**
Resources **231**
Index **235**

ROUTES AT A GLANCE

	Route	Mileage	Ride Type	Technical Difficulty	Fitness Intensity
1.	Page Meadows	9.2	Loop	Intermediate	Moderate
2.	Scott Peak	17.5	Out-and-back	Intermediate	Strenuous
3.	Stanford Rock	13.9	Loop	Expert	Very strenuous
4.	Glass Mountain	9	Loop	Advanced	Moderate
5.	Antone Meadows and Whoop-de-doo	9.5	Loop	Beginner	Easy
6.	Painted Rock	12.5	Loop	Intermediate	Moderate
7.	Watson Lake	16.9	Loop	Advanced	Strenuous
8.	Missing Link	7.1	Lollipop loop	Advanced	Moderate
9.	Mount Watson	17.1	Loop	Expert	Strenuous
10.	OTB (Over the Bars)	13.9	Lollipop loop	Intermediate	Strenuous
11.	Brockway Summit to Tahoe City	20.1	Shuttle	Advanced	Strenuous
12.	Squaw Valley Downhill	3.8	Loop	Intermediate	Easy
13.	Mount Baldy	14.3	Out-and-back	Advanced	Strenuous
14.	Kings Beach Trails	8	Shuttle	Intermediate	Easy
15.	Tyrolean Downhill	4.2	Shuttle	Advanced	Easy
16.	Mount Rose to Chimney Beach	20.5	Shuttle	Advanced	Strenuous
17.	Marlette Peak	23.4	Shuttle	Advanced	Strenuous
18.	Flume Trail	13.6	Shuttle	Beginner	Moderate
19.	The Bench	24.2	Out-and-back	Expert	Very strenuous
20.	Sierra Canyon *Spooner* *Kingsbury*	18.1 16.5	Shuttle	Expert	Moderate
21.	Monument Pass	24.9	Loop	Expert	Very strenuous
22.	Cold Creek to Star Lake	16	Out-and-back	Expert	Strenuous
23.	Freel Pass	23.3	Loop	Expert	Very strenuous
24.	Van Sickle Trail	9.3	Loop	Advanced	Moderate

Route	Mileage	Ride Type	Technical Difficulty	Fitness Intensity
25. Mr. Toad's Wild Ride	19.4	Loop	Expert	Strenuous
26. Big Meadow to Kingsbury South	22	Shuttle	Expert	Very strenuous
27. Powerline Trail	6.6	Out-and-back	Beginner	Easy
28. Corral Trails	8.1	Loop	Intermediate	Moderate
29. Christmas Valley	8.4	Loop	Expert	Strenuous
30. Gun Mount Trail	12	Out-and-back	Beginner	Easy
31. Tahoe Mountain	7.8	Loop	Intermediate	Moderate
32. General Creek	9.8	Out-and-back	Beginner	Easy
33. Jackass Ridge	4.1	Loop	Intermediate	Easy
34. Hole in the Ground	15.8	Loop	Expert	Moderate
35. Donner Lake Rim Trail	15.6	Out-and-back	Advanced	Strenuous
36. Euer Valley	8.6	Loop	Intermediate	Easy
37. Prosser Hill	6.9	Loop	Intermediate	Strenuous
38. Emigrant Trail	18.2	Out-and-back	Beginner	Moderate
39. Lloyds Loop	5.8	Loop	Intermediate	Easy
40. Sawtooth Ridge	10.5	Lollipop loop	Intermediate	Moderate
41. Downieville	15	Shuttle	Expert	Moderate
42. Mills Peak	17.6	Out-and-back	Advanced	Strenuous
43. Scotts Flat Trail	9.2	Loop	Beginner	Easy
44. Pioneer Trail	16.8	Out-and-back	Beginner	Moderate
45. Foresthill Divide	16.8	Lollipop loop	Intermediate	Moderate
46. Sly Park and Jenkinson Lake	8.8	Loop	Beginner	Easy
47. Fleming Meadow	8	Loop	Beginner	Moderate
48. Peavine Peak: Keystone Canyon to Bacon Strip	9.8	Loop	Intermediate	Moderate
49. Kings Canyon to Ash Canyon	14.4	Loop	Intermediate	Strenuous
50. Clear Creek Trail	19.4	Out-and-back	Intermediate	Moderate

ACKNOWLEDGMENTS

I would like to acknowledge the hard work and dedication of the many groups and individuals tirelessly working to maintain, improve, and expand the trails in the Lake Tahoe area. I offer a huge thank you to my beautiful wife for her support and understanding during the process of writing this guide-book, to all of my friends and family, and especially to everyone I've shared the trail with over the years. And I cannot sufficiently express my gratitude to Olympic Bike Shop, Clif Bar, Smith Optics, Deuter, and Adventure Medical Kits for their generous support during this project.

Opposite: *Spinning over a dirt jump at the Truckee Bike Park* (Hazen Woolson)

WELCOME TO LAKE TAHOE

Nestled high in the Sierra Nevada, straddling the California-Nevada state line, is a scene so beautiful that Mark Twain called it "surely the fairest picture the whole world affords." Lake Tahoe's clear blue waters, framed by the Sierra Nevada to the west and the Carson Range to the east, make it easy to understand why it is known as the Jewel of the Sierra and the Lake of the Sky.

The lake and the mountains that encircle it are a recreational paradise for local residents and the millions of visitors who come from around the world each year to hike, rock climb, kayak, stand-up paddleboard, snowboard, ski, and, of course, mountain bike. The mountains surrounding the lake are home to a vast network of trails, which, when coupled with the outrageously beautiful backdrop of Lake Tahoe itself, make for a mountain biking paradise.

GROWING AND MAINTAINING THE LAKE TAHOE TRAIL SYSTEM

With literally hundreds of miles of trails open to mountain bikes and with rides to suit all ability and fitness levels, the Lake Tahoe area truly is an incredible place to ride a mountain bike. As the sport continues to grow in popularity, the area is becoming increasingly mountain bike friendly with ongoing improvements and expansion of the trail network. These efforts are due to the hard work and advocacy of groups like the US Forest Service, Tahoe Area Mountain Biking Association (TAMBA), Tahoe Rim Trail Association, Truckee Trails Foundation, Tahoe Donner Association, Truckee Donner Land Trust, Sierra Buttes Trail Stewardship, Poedunks, Muscle Powered,

Opposite: *Dropping down near the junction with the Tahoe Rim Trail at Star Lake below Jobs Sister*

Descending an exposed section of the First Divide Trail in Downieville

and Bicyclists of Nevada County to name just a few, along with volunteers and monetary contributors. There has never been a better time to be a mountain biker in the Lake Tahoe area, and it just keeps getting better.

The 165-mile Tahoe Rim Trail (TRT) circumnavigates the lake along the spines of the Sierra and Carson ranges that surround it and serves as the backbone of Tahoe's trail skeleton. Over the course of the TRT, numerous other trails and roads intersect it, creating endless options for loops of various lengths, point-to-point rides, and all-day epics. Construction of this multi-use trail began in 1984 and was completed eighteen years later in the fall of 2001. "The TRT was originally envisioned as a hiking and equestrian trail," says TRT Association executive director Mary Bennington. "In 1984 there weren't that many people mountain biking, but over the years as mountain biking became more popular, sections of the trail were opened to bikes." Now, roughly one hundred miles of the TRT are open to mountain biking and offer some of the finest riding in the Tahoe basin, with beautiful singletrack that contours, climbs, and descends the ridges and mountains surrounding the lake. In those one hundred miles, the trail offers the full spectrum of terrain, topography, technical challenge, geology, flora, and fauna that you can find around the lake. Long climbs lead to vistas that will take your breath away, literally, and to descents that will thrill riders of all ability levels.

Roughly 80 percent of the lands within the Tahoe basin are public lands managed by the US Forest Service Lake Tahoe Basin Management Unit (USFS LTBMU). On those lands are 349 total miles of trail, 194 of which are managed for mountain bike use. The USFS is primarily responsible for all trail work that takes place on National Forest lands and employs a full-time trail crew to handle the task, but they don't go it alone. "We are very lucky to have amazing partners in Tahoe relative to mountain biking trails," says Garrett Villanueva, assistant forest engineer for the USFS LTBMU. "The Tahoe Rim Trail Association and TAMBA have been extremely helpful in the process of creating and maintaining area trails through countless volunteer hours."

"Community involvement just keeps increasing," says TAMBA president Ben Fish. "We have momentum and good things are happening all around the lake." TAMBA has proven to be very effective at involving the local community and in 2014 had 86 trail workdays involving 363 volunteers for a total of 3905 volunteer hours. When it was founded in 1988, TAMBA worked tirelessly to advocate for the sport and gain recognition with land managers as a user group on area trails. This group of dedicated individuals helped shape the future of mountain biking in Lake Tahoe during the sport's adolescence. By the mid-2000s, however, interest in the group had faded and it lay dormant for several years until its resurgence in early 2011. "We are lucky to have a good working relationship with the USFS and we are at a point where we can effectively instigate trail projects," says Fish. "We also have trail crew leaders who are trained in cooperation with the USFS, which allows us to do trail work without their direct supervision."

"One of our goals is to provide for a trail system that matches the demographic that uses the trails," says the LTBMU's Villanueva. "Mountain bikers are a growing portion of that demographic." Nowhere is this more evident than in South Lake Tahoe, where recent work on the Corral Trails has showcased the cooperative efforts of the USFS, TAMBA, and the local mountain biking community. During the summer of 2015, a number of freeride mountain bike features were built on the Lower Corral Trail, making it one of the first trails in the country to be designed and constructed by the USFS.

Likewise, in Truckee, groups like the Truckee Trails Foundation and the Truckee Donner Land Trust are helping to maintain and create new trails

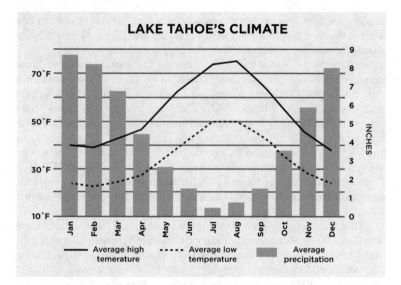

LAKE TAHOE'S CLIMATE

Legend: Average high temerature · Average low temperature · Average precipitation

while preserving open space. In Downieville, California, the Sierra Buttes Trail Stewardship has shouldered the responsibility for creating and maintaining the amazing trails in that area. Mountain biking in the Tahoe region is already incredible, and it is only getting better.

ABOUT THE LAKE TAHOE REGION

First, a few fun facts about the lake. At 22 miles long, 12 miles wide, and with 72 miles of shoreline, Lake Tahoe is the largest alpine lake in North America. And, at 1645 feet deep with an average depth of 1000 feet, it is the second deepest lake in the United States and the tenth deepest in the entire world. Lake Tahoe is fed by numerous streams that flow down from the mountains around the lake, but it has only one outlet, the Truckee River. Water spills out of Lake Tahoe and into the Truckee River through a small dam in Tahoe City before continuing northeast through Truckee, Reno, and on to Pyramid Lake.

Climate

Most of the annual precipitation in the Lake Tahoe region falls as snow during the winter months—November through April—with an average of the equivalent of fifty-five inches of precipitation falling on the mountains on

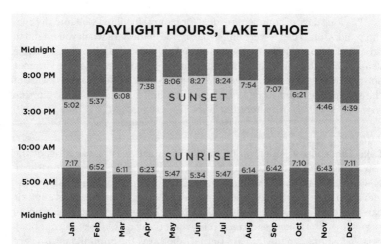

DAYLIGHT HOURS, LAKE TAHOE

Source: Lake Tahoe Basin Trail Map, Adventure Maps, 2015. Note: Times are for the fifteenth of each month and adjusted for daylight savings.

the west side of the lake and roughly half that on the mountains on the lake's east side. Snowmelt usually occurs during late spring and early summer, so the riding season for trails in the Lake Tahoe area is generally June through October, although it varies based on the snowpack, elevation, and aspect of the trail in question. Some years the high-elevation trails may be blocked by snow well into July, while during others they may be clear in early May. Likewise, on light snow years it is possible, although somewhat uncommon, for some low-elevation trails to be rideable nearly year round. Generally, very little rain falls during the summer months, although infrequent rain showers and thunderstorms do occur, providing the trails with much-needed moisture.

During the mountain biking season, the average daily temperatures are reflective of the mountain environment and are ideal for outdoor recreation. Daytime highs rarely reach the nineties, even during the hottest months of July and August, and overnight lows rarely dip below the forties and fifties. Humidity is usually very low; however, the sun feels intense at this elevation and it may often seem much warmer. Remember that these are just averages; freezing temperatures and snowfall can occur during any month of the year in the Lake Tahoe area so please pay attention to the weather and be prepared for anything while out on the trails.

The long days of summer are ideal for mountain biking well into the evening, and while it can be very enjoyable to ride in the dark when you intend to do so and are prepared with the appropriate lights and clothing, most people generally try to avoid riding once the sun has gone down. After the summer solstice in late June the days get progressively shorter, so please be aware of the approximate sunset time when you are riding to avoid finishing your ride in the dark, unless, of course, that is your intention.

Altitude

Lake Tahoe sits at an elevation of 6225 feet above sea level. Most of the routes included in this book (with the exception of the rides in the Sierra Nevada foothills and Reno and Carson City sections) occur at or above this elevation to as high as 9700 feet. For riders visiting from lower elevations it can take days or weeks to fully acclimate to the elevation, especially while exercising. Start slowly and ease into your efforts on the bike as your body gets accustomed to the thin air. In the Tahoe area the humidity is also very low, and the sun very intense, so be sure to bring and drink plenty of water and wear sunscreen when riding. Altitude sickness is relatively uncommon at these elevations, but anyone experiencing symptoms like headaches, nausea, and shortness of breath will generally find relief by descending in elevation and resting.

Flora and Fauna

The forests around the lake are an ideal home for a variety of animals such as black bears, coyotes, bobcats, squirrels, marmots, and deer. It is possible that you may spot any number of these animals while out on the trail. More often than not you will notice them as they are running away from you as quickly as they can since all of these animals are far more afraid of you than you are of them. That being said, always keep your distance, don't feed them, and do your best to avoid getting between a momma bear and her cubs. Mountain lions are occasionally spotted in the greater Tahoe area, but these sightings are extremely rare. The treetops and skies are also full of life and it is not uncommon to see a great diversity of birds, including red-tailed hawks, bald eagles, ravens, mergansers, ducks, Canadian geese, Steller's jays, Clark's nutcrackers, tanagers, and mountain chickadees.

The forests and meadows of the region also support an incredible array of plant life. Made up primarily of varieties of pine, fir, hemlock, and cedar trees, the forests are interrupted with occasional groves of aspen that light up in the

High above Carson City on the Ash to Kings Trail between Kings Canyon and Ash Canyon

fall. Several different types of bushes such as manzanita, tobacco brush, and whitethorn cover the forest floor, while in the alpine and high desert meadows feature varieties of sagebrush, rabbitbrush, and grasses. Throughout the region wildflowers of every color and size bloom during the summer, creating a feast for the eyes and a serious distraction for flower-loving cyclists. There are far too many to name them all here, but some of the more commonly seen are wooly mule-ears, arrowleaf balsamroot, Indian paintbrush, wallflower, snowplants, pinedrops, columbine, and numerous varieties of lupine, gilia, lily, and penstemon. Those with an appreciation for the natural beauty of wildflowers are truly in for a treat at the right time of year.

GEAR

The sport of mountain biking is only a few decades old. What started in the late 1970s and early 1980s as riding on dirt roads on modified beach cruisers, known as "klunkers," has quickly evolved into the sport that we know today. Mountain bike technology is now advancing so rapidly that it is hard to stay on top of the latest gear and trends. Our sport now has three wheel sizes—26-inch, 27.5-inch, and 29-inch—and bikes made for every discipline in aluminum or carbon fiber. There are also plus-sized wheels and tires, fat bikes for riding in the snow, and more options than you could possibly imagine. You could easily spend over ten thousand dollars on a mountain bike if you so choose. There has never been a better time to be a mountain biker, but it's not all about having the fanciest or newest bike out there. The best mountain bike is the one you have, so take good care of it and most importantly, get out and ride it! That said, for the routes in this book, I strongly recommend a modern mountain bike with front or full suspension and knobby mountain bike tires at least two inches wide.

In addition to your bike, it's important to have a number of other things with you when you ride. When you go for a mountain bike ride you are responsible for your own safety and the safety of your group. You may not encounter other trail users over the course of your entire ride so you need to plan to be self-sufficient. The first items that should go in your gear bags are the Ten Essentials, as developed by The Mountaineers:

1. Navigation (map and compass)
2. Sun protection (sunglasses and sunscreen)
3. Insulation (appropriate clothing and layers)
4. Illumination (headlamp or flashlight)
5. First-aid supplies
6. Fire (firestarter and matches or lighter)
7. Repair kit and tools (including knife; see detailed bike-specific list below)
8. Nutrition (extra food; quantity depends on ride duration)
9. Hydration (extra water in a hydration pack or water bottles)
10. Emergency shelter

It is also very important to know how to perform small repairs like changing a tube in a flat tire or fixing a broken chain. You won't be able to fix every mechanical problem or address every injury that you experience out on the trail, but with the items listed below you will be able to handle the majority of

Crossing the bridge in Big Meadow en route to the Christmas Valley Trail

common problems that occur. Additionally, depending on the weather or the duration of my planned ride, here is what I bring:

- Helmet
- Eye protection (sport glasses or sunglasses)
- Gloves
- Shoes: Mountain-bike-specific shoes are preferred, but sturdy closed-toe shoes will do.
- Padded shorts

And in my tool kit I make sure I have:

- Multi-tool: One that includes Allen wrenches, a torx wrench, screw-drivers, and a chain tool.
- Quick link: For quick and easy fix of a broken chain.
- Two tubes appropriately sized for your bike and tires: Because some-times you get two flats.
- Patch kit: Because sometimes you get more than two flats.
- Tire levers

- Tubeless tire plugs: Using these can be easier and faster than putting in a tube.
- Tire pump or quick-fill CO_2 cartridges
- Shock pump (optional)
- Small bottle of lube: For mid-ride chain lubing.
- Zip ties, various sizes: Handy for all kinds of things.
- Small roll of duct tape

For cooler weather riding I bring:
- Windbreaker: Lightweight and packable
- Arm warmers
- Knee warmers
- A thin headband or hat: Fits under my helmet to cover my ears.

BEFORE YOU GO

Any good ride starts with a plan. Choose a ride that is appropriate for the skill and fitness levels of all members of your group. Check with local shops for current trail conditions, especially early and late in the season when snow may be a concern, and be sure to check the local weather so you can plan and dress accordingly. Let someone know where you are going and when you expect to return. Perform a pre-ride bike check to ensure that your bike is in good and safe working order. A basic check includes making sure that wheels are attached properly, tires are at the correct air pressure, and your brakes are functioning and gears are shifting properly. If you are unsure, have an expert at a local bike shop look over your bike for you.

Rules of the Trail

To be prepared, you also need to know the rules of the trail. The International Mountain Bicycling Association (IMBA) developed these rules to promote responsible and courteous conduct on shared-use trails. Mountain biking is fun, but it can be a contentious issue with other trail users. Please do your part to help maintain mountain bike access by obeying the rules listed below:

Ride open trails: Respect trail and road closures. Ask a land manager for clarification if you are uncertain about the status of a trail. Do not trespass on private land. Obtain permits or other authorization as required. Be aware that bicycles are not permitted in areas protected as state or federal wilderness.

Leave no trace: Be sensitive to the dirt beneath you. Wet and muddy trails are more vulnerable to damage than dry ones. When the trail is soft, consider other riding options. This also means staying on existing trails and not creating new ones. Don't cut switchbacks. Be sure to pack out at least as much as you pack in.

Control your bicycle: Inattention for even a moment could put you and others at risk. Obey all bicycle speed regulations and recommendations and ride within your limits.

Yield appropriately: Do your utmost to let your fellow trail users know you're coming—a friendly greeting or bell ring are good methods. Try to anticipate other trail users as you ride around corners. Bicyclists should yield to other nonmotorized trail users unless the trail is clearly signed for bike-only travel. Bicyclists traveling downhill should yield to ones headed uphill unless the trail is clearly signed for one-way or downhill-only traffic. In general, strive to make each pass a safe and courteous one.

Never intentionally scare animals: Animals are easily startled by an unannounced approach, a sudden movement, or a loud noise. Give animals enough room and time to adjust to you. When passing horses, use special care and follow directions from the horseback riders (ask if uncertain). Running cattle and disturbing wildlife are serious offenses.

Plan ahead: Know your equipment, your ability, and the area in which you are riding and prepare accordingly. Strive to be self-sufficient: Keep your equipment in good repair and carry necessary supplies for changes in weather or other conditions. Always wear a helmet and appropriate safety gear.

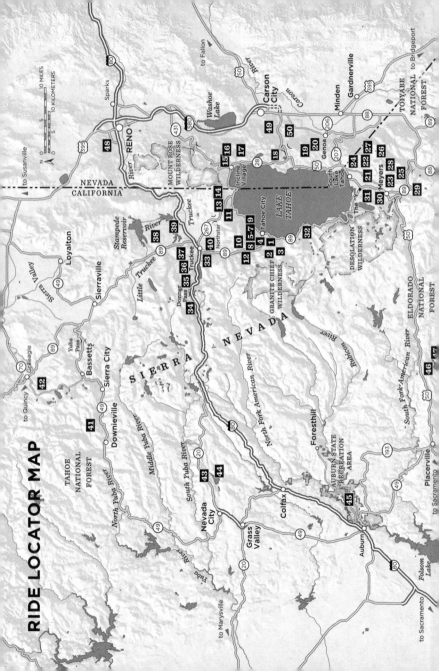

HOW TO USE
THIS GUIDE

The routes are grouped together by geographic region, circling the lake clockwise, starting from Tahoe City and finishing on the west shore near Tahoma before moving on to Truckee, Downieville, and Graeagle, and then to a handful of rides in the west slope foothills and in the Reno and Carson City areas.

Each route description starts with an information block that provides a quick reference to the basics and then moves on to a more detailed description, including a turn-by-turn mileage log and some options for changing up the ride. Below the route title, each one is labeled as either an out-and-back, loop, lollipop (partial) loop, or shuttle ride. A map for every ride shows the parking area, major roads, described route, and intersecting trails. You'll find the following data in the information block.

TRAIL TYPE
This describes the types of trail and lists the percentage of each on a given route.

DISTANCE
The distances of rides have been calculated using a GPS receiver and are as accurate as possible. Since GPS technology isn't 100 percent accurate, don't be surprised if your numbers vary slightly from those in the route descriptions.

ELEVATION GAIN/LOSS
Described in vertical feet, this is calculated using GPS and rounded to the nearest ten-foot increment. The gain and loss for all loops and out-and-back

Tackling the technical rock gardens of the Donner Lake Rim Trail above Interstate 80 near Donner Summit

rides will always be the same, while gain and loss for point-to-point rides and shuttles usually will differ, with loss usually exceeding the gain.

HIGH POINT
Every route lists the highest point of the ride.

RIDE TIME
Ride times are approximate and are listed as a range in hours. The range is calculated based on the fastest known time to complete the ride for the low end and roughly double that for the high end. For example, a fit, expert rider

may average ten or more miles per hour over the course of a ride, while an intermediate rider may average five miles per hour for the same ride.

DIFFICULTY RATINGS

The overall difficulty of these routes has been broken down into two separate categories, one for technical challenge and one for fitness intensity. While they often go hand in hand, many times they do not. Hopefully these ratings will serve to help you make informed decisions to find rides that match your ability and fitness levels for a more pleasurable experience on the trails.

Technical Difficulty: Routes are rated on a scale of technical difficulty based on ability level from beginner to expert. Each route's rating refers to the rider's ability level needed to negotiate the trail's obstacles while remaining on their bike. Bear in mind that in many cases the technical challenges of a route are limited to short sections and it may be possible for the rider to either ride around the section (as with the jumps on the Lower Corral Trail, for example) or get off and walk. It is also worth noting that in the advanced-and expert-level rides there are some obstacles that are too difficult to ride, either up or down; these are considered hike-a-bike sections and most, if not all, riders walk them.

A NOTE ABOUT SAFETY

Safety is an important concern in all outdoor activities. No guidebook can alert you to every hazard or anticipate the limitations of every reader. The descriptions of roads, trails, routes, and natural features in this book are not representations that a particular place or excursion will be safe for your party or appropriate for their level of skill and experience. As such, all users of this guide assume any and all risks associated with riding a mountain bike on the routes and terrain described herein. Safety is solely your responsibility: Under normal conditions, mountain bike excursions require the usual attention to traffic, road and trail conditions, weather, terrain, the capabilities of your party, and other factors. Always wear a properly fitting helmet and be prepared to deal with changing weather, mechanical issues, and first-aid needs on the trail. Keep informed on current conditions and exercise common sense for a safe, enjoyable outing. The publisher and author are not responsible for any adverse consequences resulting directly or indirectly from information contained in this book.

—*Mountaineers Books*

Catching a little air off one of the waterbars on the Whoop-de-doo Trail
(Heather Benson)

Technical difficulty has been broken down into four ratings: beginner, intermediate, advanced, and expert. It is important to understand what category you fall into and to ride according to your ability level.

- **Beginner:** Featuring easy trails that are generally flat, smooth, and stable, beginner routes often have a wider trail tread and few obstacles or steep sections.
- **Intermediate:** Trail tread on intermediate routes is rougher and narrower, with occasional smaller, generally rollable, unavoidable obstacles, and steeper sections of trail.
- **Advanced:** With narrow and often uneven trail tread and slightly steeper grades, advanced trails also have unavoidable obstacles in the trail—such as rocks, roots, and loose soil—that require more advanced techniques to negotiate.
- **Expert:** Expert trails have nearly continuously uneven trail tread with a steady menu of rocks, roots, and loose dirt. These trails feature steeper grades and larger unavoidable obstacles in the trail, including rollovers, small drops, possible exposure, and long, challenging rock gardens. These trails may also include short sections of hike-a-bike for most riders.

Fitness Intensity: When selecting a route, it is also important to pay attention to its rating, which is based on a scale of effort that is quantified by both distance and vertical feet of climbing. Often both the distance and vertical gain will fall into the same effort rating, but many times they will not. In these cases, the route will always have the more difficult of the two ratings. For example, if a ride is only 9 miles but with 1250 feet of vertical gain, it would be rated as moderate. These ratings are subjective and dependent on your fitness level, acclimation, and the effort you put forth.

- **Easy:** 10 miles or less and/or 1000 or less feet of vertical gain.
- **Moderate:** 10 to 15 miles and/or 1000 to 2000 feet of vertical gain.
- **Strenuous:** 15 to 25 miles and/or 2000 to 3000 feet of vertical gain.
- **Very strenuous:** 25-plus miles and/or over 3000 feet of vertical gain.

SEASON

The riding season in the Lake Tahoe region can vary wildly from year to year, depending on the winter weather and snowpack; therefore, the season listed for each route is only a rough guideline. Please use common sense and be

Riding the narrow sidehill singletrack near the top of the OTB trail (Heather Benson)

sure to check with local shops and land management agencies for the most current trail conditions, especially early and late in the season.

MAP

Each map in this book provides the best and most current information available for the suggested route. The Adventure Maps Lake Tahoe Basin Trail Map is the most useful map for nearly all mountain trails in the Tahoe basin and the Truckee area. USGS 7.5-minute maps are also listed for reference; however, they likely do not have the most current trails on them.

GPS

Loop rides and out-and-back rides show GPS coordinates for the route's trailhead. Shuttle rides have coordinates for both the start and finish. GPS coordinates are listed in degrees, minutes, and decimal seconds, using the WGS84 datum (for example: 39°9′50.69″ N, -120°8′50.79″ W).

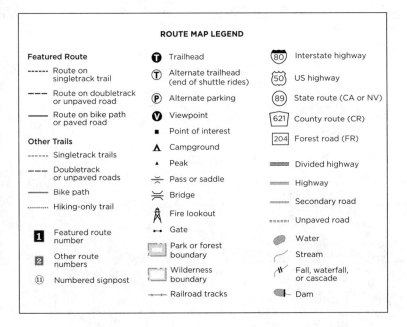

ROUTE MAP LEGEND

Featured Route

- - - - - - Route on singletrack trail
- - - Route on doubletrack or unpaved road
——— Route on bike path or paved road

Other Trails

- - - - - - Singletrack trails
- - - Doubletrack or unpaved roads
——— Bike path
·········· Hiking-only trail

1 Featured route number

2 Other route numbers

⑪ Numbered signpost

T Trailhead

T Alternate trailhead (end of shuttle rides)

P Alternate parking

V Viewpoint

■ Point of interest

▲ Campground

▲ Peak

Pass or saddle

Bridge

Fire lookout

•—• Gate

Park or forest boundary

Wilderness boundary

+—+—+ Railroad tracks

(80) Interstate highway

(50) US highway

(89) State route (CA or NV)

621 County route (CR)

204 Forest road (FR)

Divided highway

Highway

Secondary road

Unpaved road

Water

Stream

Fall, waterfall, or cascade

Dam

BEYOND THE INFO BLOCK

You'll find a brief description of the route and its highlights in the **Overview** and complete driving directions to the trailhead under **Getting There**. Additionally, the **Mileage Log** details the route's turns, intersections, and points of interest from start to finish. Look in **Options** to find out how the route can be altered.

It is important to note that these routes simply reflect my recommendations on how to approach the trails in the greater Lake Tahoe area. There is virtually no limit to the ways these trails can be ridden and linked together to create routes of various lengths and difficulties. Please use this guidebook as a starting point and as a reference to learn about the trails. I urge you to continue exploring from there.

NORTH LAKE TAHOE

(TAHOE CITY TO KINGS BEACH)

Stretching northeast from Tahoe City to Kings Beach and west to Alpine Meadows and Squaw Valley, North Lake Tahoe is a mountain biker's dream. Tahoe City is centrally located in this region and is home to a small population of full-time residents and a high percentage of hardcore mountain bikers. Paved bike paths extend from Tahoe City in all directions, providing easy access to a number of trails, including the Tahoe Rim Trail (TRT), which serves as the main artery of North Lake Tahoe's mountain biking trail system with numerous other trails and dirt roads intersecting it along its course. There is virtually no limit to the riding options around here, with more ways to link up the trails than can be mentioned in this guidebook. Be sure to pack a lot of snacks and bring your sense of adventure because there's a lot of exploring to do.

1 PAGE MEADOWS

LOOP

Trail Type: 80% singletrack, 15% pavement, 5% doubletrack
Distance: 9.2 miles
Elevation Gain/Loss: 1000/1000 feet
High Point: 7006 feet
Ride Time: 1–2 hours
Technical Difficulty: Intermediate

Fitness Intensity: Moderate
Season: Late spring–fall
Maps: Adventure Maps Lake Tahoe Basin Trail Map, 2015 version; USGS 7.5-minute Tahoe City
GPS: 39°9'50.69" N, -120°8'50.79" W

Opposite: *On the descent of Mount Watson above Tahoe City, the view can be a little distracting.*

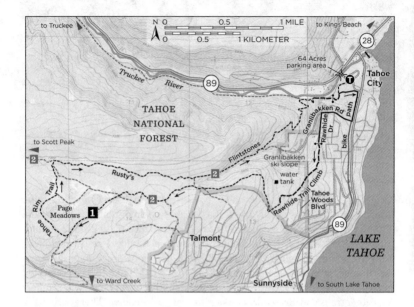

OVERVIEW

Beginning right in Tahoe City, this great, short loop showcases excellent singletrack riding for all abilities. Page Meadows is a series of interconnected meadows that offer amazing views of wildflowers in midsummer and fall foliage in October. The meadows often may be very marshy in the late spring, making for a very wet or mosquito-plagued ride, but the Tahoe Rim Trail (TRT) features a raised cinderblock trail that allows for relatively dry passage even during the wet season.

After a short climb on a bike path and neighborhood roads, the ride climbs up a fire road before turning to singletrack on an old roadbed up through the meadows. The route then joins up with the TRT to loop through the western end of the meadows before paralleling Page Meadows on a twisty, fun section of trail known as Rusty's. Finally, you'll drop down toward Tahoe City and the Truckee River on a steeper section commonly called Flintstones. There are a number of ways to lengthen this ride or to reduce the difficulty level (see Options).

GETTING THERE

The 64 Acres parking area in Tahoe City is where you will start and finish this ride, and it is also useful for several other rides in this area. From the Y intersection of CA 89 and CA 28 in Tahoe City, travel 0.3 mile south on West Lake Boulevard (CA 89) and turn west into the parking area.

MILEAGE LOG

0.0   From the parking area, ride back out to CA 89 and take a right on the bike path.

0.4   Turn right onto Granlibakken Rd.

0.6   Take the third left onto Rawhide Dr.

0.9   At the end of Rawhide Dr. continue past the closed Forest Service gate and begin the Rawhide Trail Climb.

1.5   The doubletrack climbs steadily above the Granlibakken ski and sledding slope, passes just behind a number of houses off of Tahoe Woods Blvd., and eventually turns into more of a singletrack trail on an old roadbed. Follow the main trail and continue going uphill.

2.5   The trail flattens out and becomes more rolling. There are several spur trails that branch off to the Talmont subdivision, but stay straight on the main trail.

3.5   After a gradual climb, reach a fork where the trail levels out. Bear right onto a twisting singletrack that will lead you into Page Meadows.

3.8   Turn right at the next junction, then immediately bear left. Continue straight on this trail as it crosses through the eastern side of Page Meadows before heading back into a pine forest where it drops down to a junction with the TRT.

4.4   Take a hard right onto the TRT and follow it as it climbs gently back toward the western end of the meadows.

5.0   The route exits the forest and heads back into the meadows on a raised trail with cinderblock pavers. Continue straight, passing two side trails on your right that are part of the loop around the meadows. Reenter the forest and climb slightly to a T-junction where you'll find a TRT signpost.

5.5   Turn right at the T to begin Rusty's. This rolling singletrack twists and turns its way slightly downhill to the intersection at the top of Flintstones.

6.9   Turn left at the TRT signpost to drop down the Flintstones Trail, or, for an easier descent or to lap back through the meadows, turn right here to connect with the Rawhide Trail. Flintstones starts out quite smooth

Carrying some speed through a turn on the Tahoe Rim Trail below Page Meadows and Flintstones (Heather Benson)

but quickly becomes rocky and steep at the infamous Flintstones stairs. Watch out for hikers!

7.6 At a signpost, stay on the TRT as it takes a hard left turn and head down another stretch of fun, fast trail as the TRT winds its way down to the Truckee River.

8.6 After the last switchback, stay right and continue on the singletrack of the TRT until you pop out on a gravel road.

8.9 Cross the gravel road and ride upstream along the dirt doubletrack that is directly next to the Truckee River. Stay on this doubletrack as it changes to pavement, then ride around the closed Forest Service gate.

9.2 Return to the parking area at 64 Acres.

OPTIONS

You can add extra mileage to this ride by doing laps around the meadows. But this small trail network can be a little confusing, so remember where you came from. You can also connect this ride to Route 2, Scott Peak. If you'd prefer to avoid the steep and rocky descent of Flintstones, you can return to the Rawhide Trail by taking a right after Rusty's at mile 6.9 to descend the way you came up. Those who'd prefer to warm up on the pavement can ride up from CA 89 via the bike path, Pineland Drive, and Ward Creek Boulevard to the TRT trailhead at Ward Creek.

2 SCOTT PEAK

OUT-AND-BACK

Trail Type: 90% singletrack, 10% doubletrack
Distance: 17.5 miles
Elevation Gain/Loss: 2290/2290 feet
High Point: 8280 feet
Ride Time: 2–4 hours
Technical Difficulty: Intermediate

Fitness Intensity: Strenuous
Season: Summer–fall
Maps: Adventure Maps, Lake Tahoe Basin Trail Map, 2015 version; USGS 7.5-minute, Tahoe City
GPS: 39°9′50.69″ N, -120°8′50.79″ W

OVERVIEW

Scott Peak separates the Ward and Alpine Meadows valleys just west of Tahoe City. There are several big climb-and-descent rides on this end of the lake and this is one of them. From the parking area, this route climbs 2285 vertical feet through Page Meadows and all the way up to the top of the Lakeview chair at Alpine Meadows. The climb saves the best for last as the final half mile is the steepest and most technically challenging section.

After taking in the gorgeous views of the lake, Ward Valley, and the Alpine Meadows Ski Area, drop in for a very long, and sometimes very fast, descent all the way back down to Tahoe City. Sight distance is limited in a few places, so watch your speed as you descend. While Scott Peak can be approached in a number of ways, this route provides the most time on singletrack and includes many of the same trails you'll find in Route 1, Page Meadows.

GETTING THERE

The 64 Acres parking area in Tahoe City is where you will start and finish this ride, and it is also useful for several other rides in this area. From the

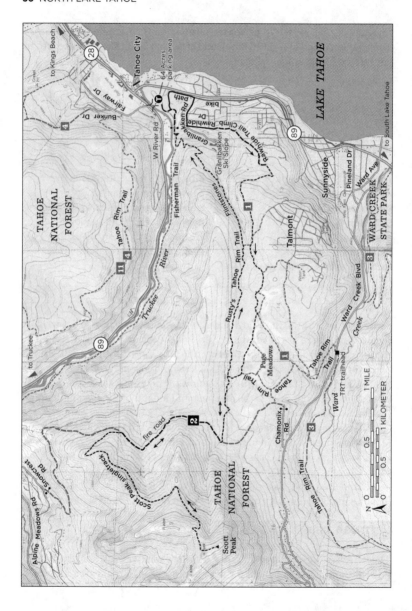

Y intersection of CA 89 and CA 28 in Tahoe City, travel 0.3 mile south on West Lake Boulevard (CA 89) and turn west into the parking area.

MILEAGE LOG

0.0 From the parking area, ride back out to CA 89 and take a right on the bike path.

0.4 Turn right onto Granlibakken Rd.

0.6 Take the third left onto Rawhide Dr.

0.9 At the end of Rawhide Dr. continue past the closed Forest Service gate and begin the Rawhide Trail Climb.

1.5 The doubletrack climbs steadily above the Granlibakken ski and sledding slope, passes just behind a number of houses off of Tahoe Woods Blvd., and eventually turns into more of a singletrack trail on an old roadbed. Follow the main trail and continue going uphill.

2.5 The trail flattens out and becomes more rolling. There are several spur trails that branch off to the Talmont subdivision, but stay straight on the main trail.

3.5 After a gradual climb, reach a fork where the trail levels out. Bear right onto a twisting singletrack that will lead you into Page Meadows.

3.8 Take a right when you hit the next trail junction, then take the next right in a couple hundred feet or so. Stay on this trail as it heads west through the meadows, offering beautiful mountain views. Stay right at any intersections.

4.4 At a T-junction with the TRT, turn right.

4.6 At the next T intersection, the TRT heads right toward the section known as Rusty's. Turn left off of the TRT and begin a gentle climb.

5.3 The singletrack ends at a fire road. Continue straight and follow the old road around a sweeping right turn and head uphill.

6.7 After contouring around the mountain on doubletrack, turn left onto the Scott Peak singletrack and continue a technically easy though somewhat steep climb.

8.7 From this point, the last 0.5 mile of the climb features numerous technical rock gardens.

9.2 At the top of the climb, continue straight, past the top of Lakeview chair and the ski patrol shack.

9.4 Reach the end of the trail and an excellent viewpoint overlooking Ward Valley and Alpine Meadows Ski Area. Turn around and drop back down the way you came.

Riding past the ski patrol shack on Scott Peak

12.0 After a high-speed descent down the Scott Peak singletrack, turn right onto the doubletrack toward Page Meadows.

13.3 After a sweeping left-hand turn, continue straight onto the singletrack.

14.0 Stay straight on the TRT to head down Rusty's.

15.2 Bear left and stay on the TRT as it drops into Flintstones.

15.9 Make a hard left at the bottom of the rocky section by the signpost to stay on the TRT.

16.9 After the last switchback, stay right on the TRT and continue to the gravel road.

17.2 Cross the gravel road and ride upstream along the dirt doubletrack that is directly next to the Truckee River. Stay on this doubletrack as it changes to pavement, then ride around the closed Forest Service gate.

17.5 Arrive at the 64 Acres parking area.

OPTIONS

You can also approach this ride from Alpine Meadows by climbing up the singletrack on an old roadbed from Snowcrest Road up to the junction with the upper Scott Peak singletrack (see mile 6.7). Those who'd prefer to warm up on the pavement can ride up from CA 89 via the bike path, Pineland Drive, and Ward Creek Boulevard to the TRT trailhead at Ward Creek.

3 STANFORD ROCK

LOOP

Trail Type: 80% singletrack, 10% doubletrack, 10% pavement
Distance: 13.9 miles
Elevation Gain/Loss: 2330/2330 feet
High Point: 8432 feet
Ride Time: 1.5–3 hours
Technical Difficulty: Expert

Fitness Intensity: Very strenuous
Season: Summer–fall
Maps: Adventure Maps, Lake Tahoe Basin Trail Map, 2015 version; USGS 7.5-minute, Tahoe City, Homewood
GPS: 39°8'3.78" N, -120°9'25.76" W

OVERVIEW

Among the locals, Stanford Rock is one of the more polarizing rides in North Lake Tahoe. People seem to either love it or absolutely hate it. So before you decide to do this ride, or bring your friends on it, ask yourself if a relentlessly long and steep climb followed by an extremely technical and rocky descent is what you like. If the answer is yes, then you'll probably love this ride. If the answer is no, then there are a number of other excellent rides nearby that probably will suit you much better. Despite this ride's overall difficulty, it is possible and somewhat common for skilled riders to complete this loop clean, meaning no dabs—push-offs with the feet—on either the climb or descent.

The ride starts innocently enough as the trail parallels Ward Creek through Ward Creek State Park. After a mile or so, the pitch ramps up and stays that way—with the exception of a couple short, flat sections and some viewpoints good for rest stops—to the top of the mountain at 8432 feet. This is one of the toughest continuous climbs in the entire Tahoe area, but the views of Ward Valley from the top of Stanford Rock are well worth it, as is the long, challenging descent to the valley below. Those with an affinity for technical riding will love the rocky, and I mean really rocky, stair step section of the Tahoe Rim Trail (TRT) on the descent to Ward Creek. In addition to tough riding, this descent offers some of the best midsummer wildflower viewing around. Once you cross the bridge over Ward Creek, which was a nice addition to the trail about ten years ago, there is a fast doubletrack that brings you back to Ward Creek Boulevard and a short return on pavement to the parking area.

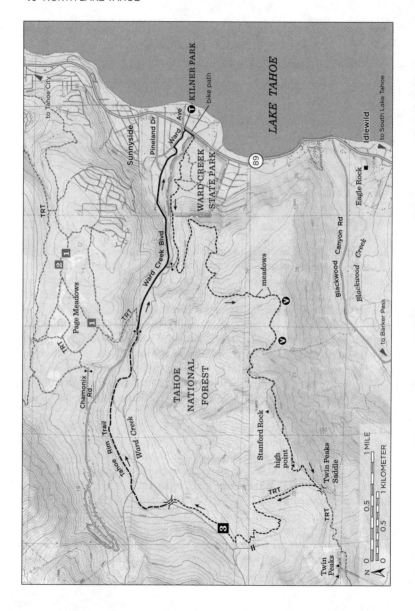

GETTING THERE

The ride begins at Kilner Park, a small, public park with free parking at the corner of CA 89 and Ward Avenue on the west shore of Lake Tahoe. Travel 3 miles south on CA 89 from Tahoe City or 24.5 miles north from the Y intersection in South Lake Tahoe.

MILEAGE LOG

0.0 Turn left out of the Kilner Park parking area, then turn right onto the bike path along CA 89.

0.2 After crossing over Ward Creek on the bike path, take the first trail you see on the right, next to the sign with information about Ward Creek State Park. This trail briefly parallels the creek.

0.5 Stay right and on the main trail at all intersections on the lower portion of this ride (for the next 0.3 mile) as you pass through Ward Creek State Park and continue climbing gently.

1.6 Take a left at the intersection (the trail to the right heads down to Ward Creek). The trail hooks right, then left, and the climb begins in earnest. The pitch of the climbing now becomes relentlessly consistent; from here to the top, the trail has an average gradient of 8 percent.

3.7 Pass through the first of two large meadows.

3.9 Pass through the second large meadow.

4.1 Just past the second meadow is a short spur trail on the left to a nice viewpoint of the lake and Blackwood Canyon.

4.5 After the trail levels out and briefly dips downhill, there is another viewpoint on the left. This is a good spot for a break as the trail only gets steeper from here.

5.4 Once you've made it up three of the steepest short climbs imaginable, the trail's relentless pitch backs off as the trail follows the ridge west.

5.9 Just as you think the climbing must be over, the trail throws one last short, but ridiculously steep, climb in for good measure.

6.2 Reach the top of the climb and an outrageous view of Twin Peaks and Ward Valley. The climbing is over; now drop in. The descent starts gradually but there are a couple turns that will sneak up on you.

6.5 This section of the descent was recently rerouted by Tahoe Area Mountain Biking Association (TAMBA) to fix a horribly loose and steep eroded descent.

Flying through a meadow of wooly mule-ears on the Tahoe Rim Trail below Twin Peaks on the Stanford Rock Loop

7.0 At the junction with the TRT at the Twin Peaks Saddle, take a hard right turn and begin a long, fast sidehill.

7.7 The trail enters a large meadow of wooly mule-ears with Twin Peaks towering high above. Once you exit this meadow, the trail becomes very rocky and technical for an extended period.

8.5 Arrive at the waterfall corner. This tough, rock-step corner is made even more challenging due to the distraction of a beautiful little waterfall. The technical riding continues; watch for sharp rock edges as they are notorious for causing pinch flat tires.

9.5 Cross the bridge over Ward Creek; the singletrack ends.

10.0 Cross another creek; there is no bridge, but it is typically dry from August on. Follow fast doubletrack from here to Ward Creek Blvd.

11.8 Ride around the Forest Service gate and turn right to return to the start of the ride.

13.4 After 1.6 miles on Ward Creek Blvd., take the first right onto Ward Ave. and follow it for 0.3 mile.

13.7 Take the next right to stay on Ward Ave. and coast down the hill.

13.9 Return to the parking area at Kilner Park.

OPTIONS

Those with an aversion to extremely rocky, technical descents can easily turn around at the Stanford Rock summit and descend the approach trail. If Stanford Rock isn't enough effort, you can easily combine this ride with the trails in the Page Meadows area to increase the distance. To reach Page Meadows, stay on the TRT at mile 11.8 instead of turning right onto Ward Creek Boulevard. You can also add a little mileage by pedaling from the TRT at the Twin Peaks Saddle at mile 7.0 up to the shoulder of Twin Peaks and back. Hardcore local riders will often combine this ride with Scott Peak (Route 2), and possibly more, for a really big day in the saddle.

4 GLASS MOUNTAIN

LOOP

Trail Type: 85% singletrack, 15% doubletrack
Distance: 9 miles
Elevation Gain/Loss: 1360/1360 feet
High Point: 7670 feet
Ride Time: 1–2 hours
Technical Difficulty: Advanced

Fitness Intensity: Moderate
Season: Late spring–fall
Maps: Adventure Maps, Lake Tahoe Basin Trail Map, 2015 version; USGS 7.5-minute, Tahoe City
GPS: 39°10′8.95″ N, -120°8′55.41″ W

OVERVIEW

An excellent stretch of the Tahoe Rim Trail (TRT), this route to Glass Mountain parallels the Truckee River canyon atop Thunder Cliff and has gained in popularity since it was rerouted a few years back to create a more scenic and less technically difficult route. This is a great ride right out of town with a moderate amount of climbing, plenty of beautiful, challenging singletrack, and stunning views of the Truckee River canyon, Squaw Valley, Alpine Meadows, Ward Valley, and Lake Tahoe.

The route climbs on fire roads and old roadbed singletrack until it joins the TRT below Glass Mountain. It also makes use of and crosses a road known as the "Fiberboard Freeway," an old logging road that stretches from Bunker Drive in Tahoe City to Brockway Summit on CA 267 between Kings Beach and Truckee. The Fiberboard Freeway is a narrow, paved road with the exception of a short stretch of dirt road between Bunker Drive and Stump

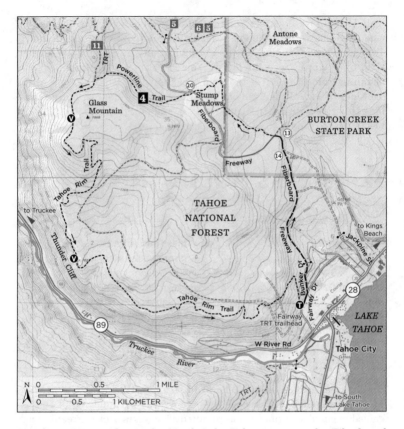

Meadows. Many rides in the North Lake Tahoe area use the Fiberboard Freeway to connect sections of trail.

There are several other ways to approach this ride and it also can easily be combined with a variety of other routes to extend the mileage (see Options).

GETTING THERE

The Fairway Drive TRT trailhead is on the western edge of Tahoe City. From the junction of CA 89 and CA 28, go west on West River Road (CA 89) for about 600 feet, and at the gas stations, turn north onto Fairway Drive. Drive

High above the Truckee River, the Tahoe Rim Trail skirts the edge of Thunder Cliff on Glass Mountain. (Heather Benson)

0.3 mile up the hill, past the fire station, and park in the Fairway Community Center parking lot, across the street from the TRT kiosk.

MILEAGE LOG

0.0 From the parking lot, turn right onto Fairway Dr.

0.1 Take the first left onto Bunker Dr. and continue uphill through the neighborhood.

0.3 After a short climb, turn left up a steep, paved driveway at the crest of the hill and pedal past several houses. This is actually the southwest end of the Fiberboard Freeway.

0.5 Continue through the Forest Service gate onto the dirt road, which is steep at times. Stay on the main road.

1.4 Ride uphill and past an unmarked road that comes in from the right until you reach an intersection with a trail map, signpost 14, on the left and a fire road on the right. This road comes from Jackpine St. in downtown Tahoe City and is an alternate way to this point. Continue straight.

1.6 After a short, steep paved section of road, arrive at a four-way intersection where you will see another trail map, signpost 13. Go straight onto a singletrack heading uphill into the forest just to the left of the signpost.

2.0 The steep, rocky singletrack climb levels out in an area known as Stump Meadows. Stay right at the first intersection and enjoy a break in the climbing.

2.3 Turn left at the next intersection at signpost 20. This trail twists and turns its way back to the Fiberboard Freeway. If you start going downhill, you missed the turn.

2.6 Go straight across the Fiberboard Freeway and pick up the Powerline Trail singletrack on the other side. This trail follows an old roadbed and a buried utility line for 0.9 mile.

3.5 At the T-junction with the TRT, turn left and begin the final bit of climbing to Glass Mountain.

4.0 The trail begins to level out and the views open up to the right (west).

4.4 Reach the top of Glass Mountain, 7670 feet. It's mostly downhill from here.

6.2 After some excellent trail, reach the unofficial halfway point of the descent. This is a great spot atop the Thunder Cliff with awesome views to rest and regroup.

6.6 Make a short climb before the trail continues its gradual, but very rocky, descent back toward Tahoe City. Lake Tahoe will occasionally come into view along the way.

8.3 Cross a dirt fire road.

8.5 Cross a second dirt fire road. The trail becomes faster and smoother than it has been. People often hike this stretch of the trail, so heads up.

9.0 After a couple of exciting rock gardens, the last three turns are steep and tight before the trail spits you out right back where you started. Watch for cars!

OPTIONS

For a more challenging ascent, it is possible to ride Glass Mountain as an out-and-back along the TRT. The first mile or so of the climb is quite steep before the pitch eases up for the duration of the climb. You can also start from Tahoe City by climbing up Jackpine Street and joining this route at 1.4 miles. Longer loops can be made with the Nordic center trails in Burton Creek State Park and with sections of the TRT farther northeast. Glass Mountain can also be ridden as a loop starting from CA 89 between Alpine Meadows and Squaw Valley and riding up the Western States Trail to the Wall to the TRT and returning on the bike path along the Truckee River.

5 ANTONE MEADOWS AND WHOOP-DE-DOO

LOOP

Trail Type: 80% singletrack, 15% doubletrack, 5% pavement
Distance: 9.5 miles
Elevation Gain/Loss: 700/700 feet
High Point: 7130 feet
Ride Time: 1–2 hours
Technical Difficulty: Beginner

Fitness Intensity: Easy
Season: Late spring–fall
Maps: Adventure Maps, Lake Tahoe Basin Trail Map, 2015 version; USGS 7.5-minute, Tahoe City, Kings Beach
GPS: 39°11'49.49" N, -120°6'22.86" W

OVERVIEW

The unofficial hub of mountain biking in North Lake Tahoe is the Nordic center, Tahoe XC, which features a maze of beginner-friendly trails and affords access to a number of excellent rides. An excellent beginner-intermediate option is this loop through Antone Meadows to the whoop-de-doos. The route primarily follows wide, mellow trails through meadows and open forest on the trails of the Nordic center and Burton Creek State Park. Recently improved signage makes this route easier to follow than it has been in the past.

From the Nordic center parking area, the route follows a doubletrack through the grassy meadows of what was once a par three golf course. A wide singletrack then heads through massive meadows of mule-ears and wildflowers before skirting north of Antone Meadows along the forest's edge. More singletrack brings you to the Fiberboard Freeway, a paved road, for a short climb to the top of the Whoop-de-doo Trail and an exciting, rolling descent. After joining back up with the doubletrack, a short pedal brings you to the Reservoir Trail and a short descent down to the dam. Cross the dam and pedal a short distance back to the neighborhood and the Nordic center.

GETTING THERE

Tahoe XC, more commonly known as the Nordic center, is located at 925 Country Club Drive in Tahoe City. From downtown Tahoe City, head

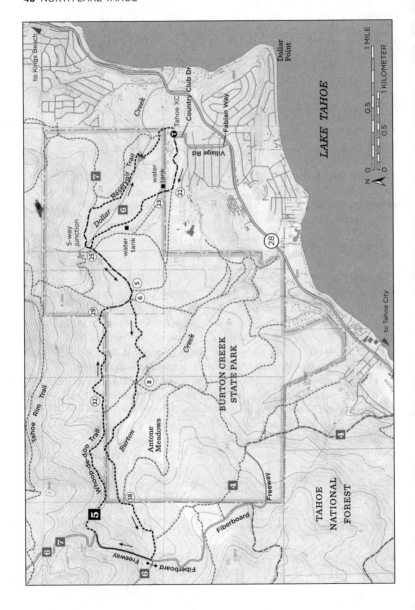

northeast on CA 28 for 2.3 miles. Just before the top of Dollar Hill, turn left (north) onto Fabian Way. Take your first right on Village Road, go straight up the hill, and follow the road around a right-hand bend. Take a left onto Country Club Drive and then turn left into the Nordic center parking lot. You can follow these same directions if pedaling from town; just ride on the bike path to the top of Dollar Hill.

MILEAGE LOG

0.0   Head west from the Nordic center on the doubletrack.

0.5   At signpost 22, turn right and ride uphill past the water tank.

0.6   Stay straight at this intersection marked with signpost 23, entering the forest on the narrower singletrack trail.

1.4   At the five-way intersection, marked with signpost 25, turn left onto the wide doubletrack and follow it west.

1.8   After a fast and slightly downhill straightaway, bear right after passing signpost 5, then immediately bear left, but not hard left, at the next intersection, signpost 6, onto the raised gravel singletrack trail. Head through a section of beautiful mule-ears meadows.

2.7   At the five-way intersection marked with signpost 8, continue straight and cruise along the northern edge of Antone Meadows on the gravel singletrack. If you find yourself on a dirt road you have gone the wrong way.

3.8   Turn right, uphill, at this intersection marked with signpost 18, and follow the singletrack, without making any turns, until you reach the Fiberboard Freeway.

4.5   Turn right on the Fiberboard Freeway and pedal uphill to the first switchback corner.

5.0   At this switchback the Whoop-de-doo Trail, aka the Jump Trail or Great Ski Race Trail, drops in; follow it east downhill. The whoop-de-doos are actually waterbars, not jumps; people love jumping off them but they don't really have landings. This trail is often gravelly and loose, and it sees uphill traffic, so pay attention.

6.2   Reach the bottom of the whoop-de-doos; continue straight past signpost 32.

7.2   Bear right at signpost 29 and continue on the doubletrack.

7.4   Bear left at the intersection, signpost 6, and get back on the doubletrack. Pass signpost 5 and make a short climb back up to the five-way intersection.

Cruising the wide trails of the Nordic center alongside Antone Meadows

8.0 Continue straight at the five-way, signpost 25, on the doubletrack. (You can also turn right here to return to the Nordic center.)

8.3 Turn onto the first singletrack you see on the right. Pay attention because it is a relatively nondescript turn. This singletrack leads down to the Dollar Creek Reservoir.

9.0 Cross the dam; there is a steep drop-off on the left, so walking your bike is recommended. Use caution.

9.1 Bear left after crossing the dam and descend the wide trail.

9.3 As the trail starts to go uphill, take the first right and immediately reach the dead end of Country Club Dr.

9.5 Arrive at the Nordic center parking area.

OPTIONS

You can explore numerous intersecting trails in the Nordic center to add mileage or make loops of various lengths. For a much longer ride, at mile 5.0 stay straight on the Fiberboard Freeway to reach the TRT. You can also do this ride in reverse if you feel like it.

6 PAINTED ROCK

LOOP

Trail Type: 60% singletrack, 30% doubletrack, 10% pavement
Distance: 12.5 miles
Elevation Gain/Loss: 1450/1450 feet
High Point: 7690 feet
Ride Time: 1.5–2.5 hours
Technical Difficulty: Intermediate

Fitness Intensity: Moderate
Season: Summer–fall
Maps: Adventure Maps, Lake Tahoe Basin Trail Map, 2015 version; USGS 7.5-minute, Tahoe City, Kings Beach
GPS: 39°11′49.49″ N, -120°6′22.86″ W

OVERVIEW

This awesome stretch of singletrack, one of the most popular sections of the Tahoe Rim Trail (TRT), lies between the Fiberboard Freeway and the top of the Wall and offers views of both the Pacific Crest and Lake Tahoe along the way. Painted Rock can be approached and incorporated into rides in a number of ways (see Options), but this route from the Nordic center is one of the easiest ways to experience this great trail.

The ride starts on the wide, mellow trails of the Nordic center before climbing up the Whoop-de-doo Trail to the Fiberboard Freeway. A short climb on pavement brings you to the TRT for a singletrack ride up and over Painted Rock. After a short and fast descent down the backside of the Wall, you'll cruise through Antone Meadows and the Nordic center trails and back to the parking area.

GETTING THERE

Tahoe XC, more commonly known as the Nordic center, is located at 925 Country Club Drive in Tahoe City. From downtown Tahoe City, head northeast on CA 28 for 2.3 miles. Just before the top of Dollar Hill, turn left (north) onto Fabian Way. Take the first right on Village Road, go straight up the hill, and follow the road around a right-hand bend. Take a left onto Country Club Drive and then turn left into the Nordic center parking lot. You can follow these same directions if pedaling from town; just ride on the bike path to the top of Dollar Hill.

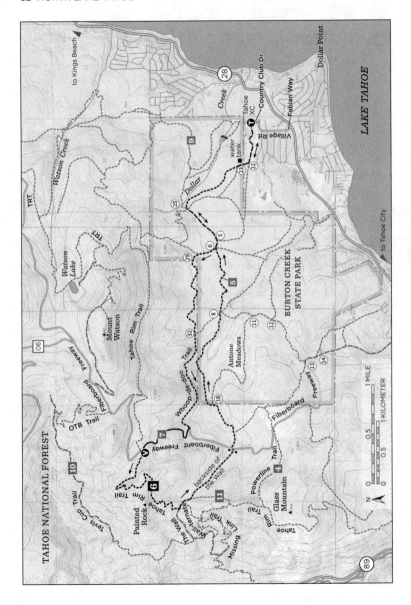

Rounding a corner on the Tahoe Rim Trail over Painted Rock (Heather Benson)

MILEAGE LOG

0.0 Head west out of the Nordic center parking area on the doubletrack.

0.5 At signpost 22 turn right and climb past the water tank.

0.6 Go straight at the intersection marked with signpost 23, and head into the forest on the narrower singletrack.

1.4 Turn left at the five-way intersection, marked with signpost 25, and follow the doubletrack.

1.9 After a fast and slightly downhill section, take a hard right once you pass signpost 5 and then continue right past signpost 6.

2.1 Turn left when the trail splits at signpost 29 and begin the rolling section of the lower Whoop-de-doo Trail.

3.1 Once you pass signpost 32, begin climbing the whoop-de-doos; watch for downhill traffic.

4.3 At the top of the Whoop-de-doo Trail, turn right to head uphill on the pavement of the Fiberboard Freeway.

5.1 Turn left on the TRT when it crosses the Fiberboard.

5.8 Take a break here and enjoy the excellent view of the Pacific Crest and Squaw Valley.

6.3 Reach the top of Painted Rock for views of Lake Tahoe. The descent begins here.

7.2 Turn left onto the doubletrack and descend the backside of the Wall. (Going straight here on the TRT leads to Missing Link and Glass Mountain; turning right on the Wall leads to the Wall-ternate and Western States Trail.)

8.0 Go around the gate at the bottom of the dirt road and travel almost directly, but slightly left, across the Fiberboard and get on the singletrack.

8.7 Turn left at this intersection, marked with signpost 18, cross the bridge, and ride along the north edge of Antone Meadows.

9.8 Bear slightly left at this intersection, signpost 8, onto the raised, crushed gravel singletrack.

10.8 Bear slightly right at signpost 6 and slightly left onto the wide doubletrack past signpost 5.

11.3 At the five-way intersection, signpost 25, bear right, not hard right, onto the singletrack that you rode in on.

12.1 Exit the forest and follow the doubletrack downhill past the water tank, then turn left at signpost 22 onto the doubletrack that leads back to the Nordic center.

12.5 Return to the Nordic center parking area.

OPTIONS

There are so many options that it's hard to name them all. First, you can go up through Antone Meadows and descend the Whoop-de-doo Trail (Route 5). You can also reverse the direction of this entire ride and go up and over Painted Rock the other way. Many people ride up to Painted Rock as an up-and-back via the Western States Trail and the Wall-ternate. For a longer ride you may want to consider riding up and over Painted Rock as described, then continuing on the TRT at mile 8.2 to Missing Link and the Western States Trail for a descent to the Truckee River and a return to Tahoe City and the Nordic center on the bike path. Painted Rock also can be incorporated into rides from either direction on the TRT (see Route 4, Glass Mountain, and Route 7, Watson Lake).

7 WATSON LAKE

LOOP

Trail Type: 70% singletrack, 25% doubletrack, 5% pavement

Distance: 16.9 miles

Elevation Gain/Loss: 1920/1920 feet

High Point: 7881 feet

Ride Time: 2–4 hours

Technical Difficulty: Advanced

Fitness Intensity: Strenuous

Season: Summer–fall

Maps: Adventure Maps, Lake Tahoe Basin Trail Map, 2015 version; USGS 7.5-minute, Tahoe City, Kings Beach

GPS: 39°11'49.49" N, -120°6'22.86" W

OVERVIEW

The Watson Lake loop has it all: tough climbs, challenging descents, one of the best views of Lake Tahoe, and the idyllic Watson Lake nestled high up beneath the summit of Mount Watson. After a mellow start on the wide trails of the Nordic center, this route contours around the east side of Mount Watson and climbs a fire road to the Tahoe Rim Trail (TRT). A bit of challenging climbing on the TRT brings you to Watson Lake before the trail wraps around to the south for a beautiful descent. You will then traverse the south side of Mount Watson before dropping down to the Fiberboard Freeway to finish on the Whoop-de-doo Trail and a mellow cruise back into the Nordic center.

GETTING THERE

Tahoe XC, more commonly known as the Nordic center, is located at 925 Country Club Drive in Tahoe City. From downtown Tahoe City, head northeast on CA 28 for 2.3 miles. Just before the top of Dollar Hill, turn left (north) onto Fabian Way. Take your first right on Village Road, go straight up the hill, and follow the road around a right-hand bend. Take a left onto Country Club Drive and then turn left into the Nordic center parking lot. You can follow these same directions if pedaling from town; just ride on the bike path to the top of Dollar Hill.

MILEAGE LOG

0.0 Head west from the Nordic center parking area on the doubletrack that climbs gently through the meadows.

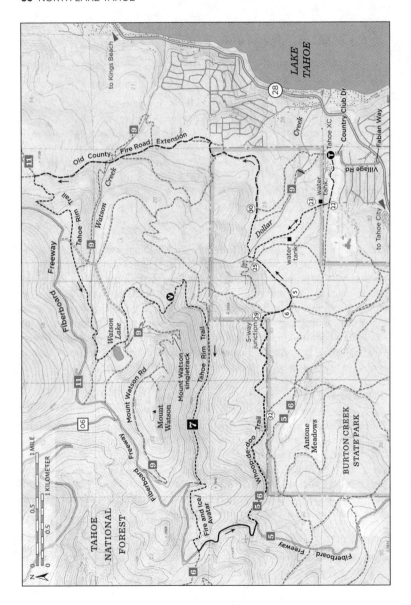

0.5 Turn right and climb past the large water tank by signpost 22.

0.6 Go straight at the intersection marked with signpost 23, and head into the forest on the narrower singletrack. This section of trail takes you past another water tank on a very gradual climb.

1.4 When you arrive at the five-way intersection, at signpost 25, turn right.

1.9 Continue straight past the top of the Reservoir Trail on the right, then at signpost 30 bear left and continue on the wide trail.

2.6 Bear left after passing through a dip in the trail onto a narrower singletrack.

2.8 Turn right at the next intersection and follow this singletrack over to a fire road.

2.9 Merge onto the Old County Fire Road Extension and turn left (north). The road dips very briefly before the climbing begins. Continue uphill on the main path of this road, not making any turns, until you reach the TRT.

4.6 Turn left on the TRT and begin climbing some technically challenging singletrack.

5.8 Ride straight across a dirt road and stay on the TRT. The trail flattens out briefly before climbing again toward Watson Lake.

7.0 Turn left at this intersection toward Watson Lake (going straight leads to the Fiberboard).

7.2 Reach Watson Lake, which is a great spot for a mid-ride break.

7.3 Ride past Watson Lake and bear left after crossing the outlet of Watson Creek; this shallow creek crossing may be dry after midsummer.

7.4 The singletrack ends at a fire road after you pass through some short wooden posts. Turn left and descend.

7.6 After passing through a large patch of gravel, pick up the singletrack on the right. This trail junction can sneak up on you and isn't that easy to see.

8.2 Ride past the bottom of the Mount Watson singletrack and begin the descent of the south side of Mount Watson. This section of trail is usually loose and gravelly.

8.5 Be sure to stop and take in the incredible view from this rocky outcrop.

9.3 Turn right at the bottom of this descent to stay on the TRT. You will climb for a few minutes before the trail flattens out and traverses west across the south side of Mount Watson.

10.7 The singletrack ends in a dirt road; turn right but look for the singletrack to continue on your left in a couple hundred feet. This is the top of the Fire and Ice/Avatar section of the TRT.

Dropping down to the shore of Watson Lake while riding the Tahoe Rim Trail
(Heather Benson)

11.7 Turn left onto the paved Fiberboard Freeway and begin to descend.

12.5 After a left switchback, look for the top of the Whoop-de-doo Trail in the large gravel turnout at the next, right, switchback. Turn left and descend the whoop-de-doos; watch for uphill traffic.

13.7 Continue straight at the bottom of the whoop-de-doos, past signpost 32.

14.7 Turn right and follow the doubletrack south at signpost 29.

14.9 Bear left at signpost 6, then left again, riding past signpost 5. Continue on the doubletrack, climbing gently back to the five-way intersection.

15.5 Back at the five-way intersection, signpost 25, take a soft right, not a hard right, and return on the same wide trail that you came up on.

16.4 Go straight at the intersection, ride downhill past the water tank, and take a left at signpost 22 to follow the doubletrack that leads back to the Tahoe XC parking area.

16.9 Arrive at the Tahoe XC parking area.

OPTIONS

There are many options along this route: You can do an up-and-back to the top of Mount Watson if you turn right on the Mount Watson singletrack at mile 8.2. By going straight on the TRT at mile 11.7, you can continue on the TRT up to Painted Rock and beyond. At mile 14.7, you can opt to turn left to do a short climb to a scenic overlook; continuing on this trail past the overlook will bring you down to the five-way intersection at signpost 25. This ride can also be done in reverse, but be advised that climbing the TRT up the south side of Mount Watson is steep and typically very loose.

8   MISSING LINK

LOLLIPOP LOOP

Trail Type: 90% singletrack, 10% doubletrack
Distance: 7.1 miles
Elevation Gain/Loss: 1500/1500 feet
High Point: 7460 feet
Ride Time: 45 minutes–1.5 hours
Technical Difficulty: Advanced

Fitness Intensity: Moderate
Season: Summer–fall
Maps: Adventure Maps, Lake Tahoe Basin Trail Map, 2015 version; USGS 7.5-minute, Tahoe City
GPS: 39°12'14.01" N, -120°12'2.57" W

OVERVIEW

For a classic downhill in North Lake Tahoe, look no further than Missing Link to Western States. The Missing Link Trail was built when slower technical descents were popular. Dropping from the TRT high above the Truckee River, Missing Link twists and turns down a steep slope with occasional exposure and many challenging rock gardens. When combined with the Western States Trail, it makes for a long descent from the ridge to the river. One of the easiest ways to approach this ride is to climb Western States and the Wall or Wall-ternate, then ride the TRT over to Missing Link and descend. This 7.1-mile lollipop loop may seem short, but the 1500 vertical feet of climbing is not to be taken lightly.

From the starting point in Squaw Valley, this route follows the bike path along the Truckee River to the Western States Trail. After climbing up the

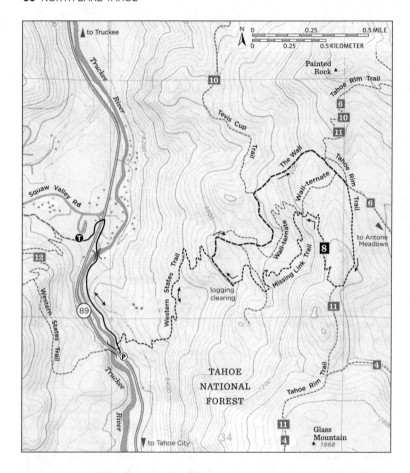

twists and turns of Western States, the climbing continues on a short, steep, fitness-testing fire road known as the Wall. At the top of the Wall, the route then follows the TRT for a short stretch over to the top of Missing Link. Drop down Missing Link, then Western States, and finish with a cruise back on the bike path to the parking area. A newer trail known as the "Wall-ternate" also leads up and down from the ridge and is an excellent singletrack alternative to the steep road of the Wall.

GETTING THERE

From Tahoe City, travel north on CA 89 for 5 miles to the junction with Squaw Valley Road. Turn west off of CA 89 onto Squaw Valley Road then take the first left into the parking area for the soccer field. You can also park in a pullout on the west side of CA 89, just south of the bridge that crosses the Truckee River 0.8 mile south of Squaw Valley Road, and start the ride from 0.8 mile in the mileage log.

MILEAGE LOG

0.0   From the parking area, cross CA 89 at the stoplight and head south on the bike path.

0.8   Take a hard left onto the singletrack Western States Trail underneath the CA 89 bridge over the Truckee River. The trail immediately starts switchbacking up the slope. Watch for downhill riders.

2.0   At the top of the Western States singletrack, turn left on the fire road and follow it as it initially dips down then climbs to the bottom of the Wall. You will pass a dirt road to the right and then the bottom of the Wall-ternate.

2.5   At the intersection with the Tevis Cup Trail, downhill to the left, turn right and begin the short, but brutally steep, climb up the Wall.

2.9   As you crest the top of the Wall, a spur trail leading to the TRT cuts left but you should continue straight instead for a gentle downhill on the fire road. Ride past the top of the Wall-ternate on the right.

3.0   Turn right on the TRT where it crosses the fire road.

3.5   Turn right onto the Missing Link Trail; the TRT continues toward Glass Mountain.

3.9   The Wall-ternate, a newer trail (see Options), joins Missing Link; stay left to continue on Missing Link. Note that this intersection can be confusing so be sure you stay on Missing Link.

4.2   A short climb breaks up the Missing Link descent.

4.6   Cross a dirt road; stay on the singletrack.

5.0   The trail ends in an old logging clearing where you will turn right onto the doubletrack. There are some fun log rides in this clearing.

5.1   Turn left onto the Western States singletrack and enjoy the winding and flowy ride back down to the bike path.

6.3   Turn right on the bike path.

7.1   Return to the parking area.

Descending the Missing Link Trail with the snowcapped peaks of Squaw Valley in the distance

OPTIONS

You can get to the top of Missing Link from the TRT in either direction and you can easily come up from the Nordic center on the other side of the ridge (see Routes 4 through 7 and 9). To add a little length to this ride, take a left at the top of the Wall at mile 2.9 and ride the TRT up to Painted Rock and back before continuing the route described above. A new trail, called the Wall-ternate, is an easier, and much more pleasant, alternative to climbing the Wall. It intersects Missing Link at mile 3.9 on the route described and reaches the TRT at about mile 3.0 of the above route (as well as via a fire road at mile 2.0 of the described route). The Wall-ternate also makes for a fun descent as yet another option.

9   MOUNT WATSON

LOOP

Trail Type: 80% singletrack, 10% doubletrack, 10% pavement
Distance: 17.1 miles

Elevation Gain/Loss: 2300/2300 feet
High Point: 8360 feet
Ride Time: 2–4 hours

Technical Difficulty: Expert
Fitness Intensity: Strenuous
Season: Summer–fall

Maps: Adventure Maps, Lake Tahoe
Basin Trail Map, 2015 version; USGS
7.5-minute, Tahoe City, Kings Beach
GPS: 39°11'49.49" N, -120°6'22.86" W

OVERVIEW

A ride to the top of Mount Watson affords one of the best lake views on the northwest end of Lake Tahoe. It's worth the pedal for the view alone, but this route also features superb riding through the Nordic center, along the Tahoe Rim Trail (TRT), and on the recently rerouted Mount Watson singletrack. Situated just east of Tahoe City atop Dollar Hill, the Nordic center is a great start and end point for this 17.1-mile loop. As with most routes, this one can be ridden in a number of ways, or incorporated into other routes, but I think the loop detailed here is the best way to check out Mount Watson and the singletrack that lies beneath it.

After a casual pedal through the mellow meadows of the Nordic center, the route starts to tick off vertical while climbing the Whoop-de-doo Trail up to the Fiberboard Freeway. After climbing the Fiberboard for a bit, the route turns onto the TRT and climbs the section known as Fire and Ice/Avatar back up to the Fiberboard Freeway. You'll then skirt around to the back side of Mount Watson where you turn onto Mount Watson Road for a short but steep dirt road climb to the top. After taking in the view among the rocks at the summit, jump on the awesome new singletrack that winds down the scenic south side of Mount Watson to its junction with the TRT. Follow the TRT past Watson Lake and then down to the Grinder Trail that parallels Watson Creek for the descent. From the bottom of the descent, you'll follow several fire roads back into the Nordic center.

GETTING THERE

Tahoe XC, more commonly known as the Nordic center, is located at 925 Country Club Drive in Tahoe City. From downtown Tahoe City, head northeast on CA 28 for 2.3 miles. Just before the top of Dollar Hill, turn left (north) onto Fabian Way. Take your first right on Village Road, go straight up the hill, and follow the road around a right-hand bend. Take a left onto Country Club Drive and then turn left into the Nordic center parking lot. You can follow these same directions if pedaling from town; just ride on the bike path to the top of Dollar Hill.

MILEAGE LOG

0.0 Head west from the Nordic center parking area on the doubletrack that climbs gently through the meadows.

0.5 At signpost 22, turn right and climb past the large water tank.

0.6 At signpost 23, continue straight at the intersection onto the narrower singletrack and into the forest. This section of trail takes you past another water tank while climbing very gradually.

1.4 Turn left at the five-way intersection, marked with signpost 25, and follow the wide cross-country ski trail as it gently goes downhill.

2.0 Bear right just past signpost 5, then take a hard right and pass signpost 6; you're now heading north through the mule-ears meadows. From here you can see the top of Mount Watson high above you.

2.2 Turn left at the fork in the trail at signpost 29. This rolling section leads to the bottom of the Whoop-de-doo Trail climb.

3.2 Continue straight past signpost 32 and begin the climb up the Whoop-de-doo Trail; be on the lookout for downhill riders.

4.5 The whoop-de-doos end in a switchback corner of the Fiberboard Freeway. Continue uphill on the Fiberboard.

5.3 Turn right onto the TRT when it crosses the road and begin the Fire and Ice/Avatar climb.

6.2 At a fire road, turn left and head back to the Fiberboard Freeway. The TRT continues to the right.

6.3 Continue uphill on the Fiberboard Freeway.

6.5 The OTB Trail drops off the Fiberboard to the left at this sweeping right turn; continue uphill on the pavement.

6.9 Take a sharp right turn onto the dirt of the Mount Watson Rd. This road starts out flat but gets progressively steeper; settle in for the climb.

8.4 At the top of the climb the singletrack is straight ahead, but the best view is just uphill to the right on a short spur road. This is a great spot for a long break. After your break, head back to the road and take a right to find the singletrack.

8.6 Get on the singletrack that drops in on the left side of the dead end of the road. Follow its winding, and somewhat gravelly, path down to the TRT.

9.9 At the T-junction with the TRT, turn left to descend toward Watson Lake.

Two riders flow down the upper section of the Mount Watson singletrack high above the Nordic Center.

10.6 Turn left when the TRT singletrack ends in a doubletrack and climb briefly.

10.8 Turn right off the doubletrack onto singletrack through the short wooden posts at the crest of the hill. Follow the singletrack across Watson Creek and skirt around the eastern edge of Watson Lake.

11.2 Turn right at the T-junction and descend this fun section of the TRT.

12.1 In a flat meadow, turn right off the TRT onto the Grinder Trail, which is marked with a 4x4 wooden post. It is the only singletrack that intersects this section of trail. If you cross the dirt road you have gone too far.

12.2 Cross a dirt road on the Grinder Trail and begin to descend more steeply. This section has a lot of sharp turns and is very rocky.

13.2 Cross the Old County Fire Road Extension.

13.9 When the singletrack ends, turn right on a fire road, cross the creek, and pedal up a short climb.

14.1 Continue straight, following the trail gently downhill, through a meadow, then continue straight and uphill.

14.6 Merge onto the Old County Fire Road Extension and follow it south, behind the neighborhood.

14.9 Bear right to stay on the main doubletrack; this will lead you back into the Nordic center.

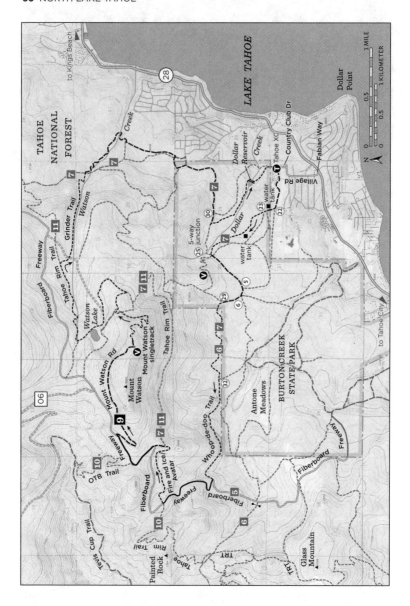

15.7 Stay right at this major intersection marked with signpost 30.

15.9 Turn left onto an unmarked singletrack. This is the Reservoir Trail, which parallels Dollar Creek and leads you to Dollar Reservoir.

16.5 Walk your bike across the reservoir's dam. Take a left once you hit the other side.

16.9 As the trail starts to go uphill, take the first right turn, which leads immediately to the dead end of Country Club Dr.

17.1 Turn right into the Nordic center parking area.

OPTIONS

A quick jaunt up to Mount Watson is often incorporated into longer rides in this area and you can easily join this route from the TRT. At mile 5.3 you can turn left on the TRT and do a quick side trip up to Painted Rock and back. After the Mount Watson singletrack, you could also turn right at mile 9.9 and follow the TRT back to Fire and Ice/Avatar and return the way you climbed up, or carry on to Route 10, OTB. You can skip the Grinder by staying on the TRT until it intersects the Old County Fire Road Extension and then rejoin the described route at mile 14.6.

10 OTB (OVER THE BARS)

LOLLIPOP LOOP

Trail Type: 65% singletrack, 25% doubletrack, 10% pavement
Distance: 13.9 miles
Elevation Gain/Loss: 2400/2400 feet
High Point: 7715 feet
Ride Time: 2–4 hours
Technical Difficulty: Intermediate

Fitness Intensity: Strenuous
Season: Summer–fall
Maps: Adventure Maps, Lake Tahoe Basin Trail Map, 2015 version; USGS 7.5-minute, Tahoe City
GPS: 39°12'14.01" N, -120°12'2.57" W

OVERVIEW

The OTB Trail is a popular stretch of singletrack that connects the Fiberboard Freeway and Tevis Cup Trail just north of Painted Rock, and riding it as a lollipop loop ties together a number of excellent trails in the area. This

14-mile ride has a bit of challenging climbing from the Truckee River up to the Tahoe Rim Trail (TRT), but this effort is handsomely rewarded with excellent descents on Painted Rock, OTB, and Western States.

After a casual warm-up spin on the Truckee River bike path, the climbing begins with the Western States Trail and the Wall or Wall-ternate to the top of the ridge and the junction with the TRT. A short climb up and over Painted Rock, across the Fiberboard, up the Fire and Ice/Avatar section of the TRT, and a short climb on the Fiberboard bring you to the top of the OTB descent. At the bottom of the OTB Trail, the Tevis Cup Trail contours around the west side of Painted Rock back to the top of Western States for a great descent back down to the Truckee River.

GETTING THERE

From Tahoe City, travel north on CA 89 for 5 miles to the junction with Squaw Valley Road. Turn west off of CA 89 onto Squaw Valley Road, then take the first left into the parking area for the soccer field. You can also park in a pullout on the west side of CA 89, just south of the bridge that crosses the Truckee River 0.8 mile south of Squaw Valley Road, and start the ride from 0.8 mile in the mileage log.

MILEAGE LOG

0.0 From the parking area, cross CA 89 at the stoplight and head south on the bike path.

0.8 Take a hard left onto the singletrack Western States Trail underneath the CA 89 bridge over the Truckee River. The trail immediately starts switchbacking up the slope. Watch for downhill riders.

2.0 At the top of the Western States singletrack, turn left on the fire road and follow it as it initially dips down then climbs over to the bottom of the Wall. You will pass a dirt road on the right and the bottom of the Wall-ternate on the way.

2.5 Turn right and begin the short, but brutally steep, climb up the Wall.

2.9 At the top of the Wall, take the first left onto singletrack and ride this very short connector trail for a few hundred feet to the TRT toward Painted Rock.

3.9 After a mile of winding singletrack climbing, top out on Painted Rock with a sliver of a lake view.

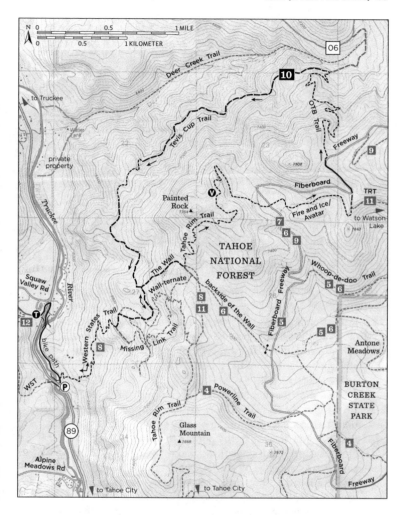

4.4 Reach a saddle with an excellent view to the west toward the Pacific Crest and Squaw Valley, then begin a descent to the Fiberboard Freeway.

Letting it run on the fast sidehill through the open forest near the top of OTB

5.1 Ride straight across the Fiberboard Freeway and begin the gradual climb up the section known as Fire and Ice/Avatar.

5.9 When the singletrack ends, turn left onto the doubletrack and stay straight to ride toward the Fiberboard Freeway as the TRT continues to the right.

6.0 Begin a short climb on the pavement of the Fiberboard Freeway.

6.3 At the end of the straightaway, as the Fiberboard begins a sweeping right turn, look for a fire road on the left; the singletrack entrance to the OTB Trail drops in to the right of this fire road. Within roughly the first 100 feet of the singletrack, you will want to stay left as another singletrack branches off to the Old OTB Trail, a moto trail. The OTB Trail is a narrow, singletrack descent with great sidehill sections and some tight, off-camber, switchback corners.

8.1 Turn left on the Tevis Cup Trail. After a very short climb this doubletrack road becomes a very fast and loose downhill, so control your speed. The doubletrack will change to singletrack for a short section before a couple of short but steep climbs that lead to the bottom of the Wall.

11.1 Turn right when you are looking up the bottom of the Wall. Follow this doubletrack back down and around to the top of the Western States Trail. You will pass the bottom of the Wall-ternate Trail and a fire road, both to your left, along the way.

11.7 Drop into the Western States Trail descent, the singletrack on your right. This is a popular trail so watch for other riders.

13.1 At the bottom of the Western States Trail take a right on the bike path.

13.9 Arrive back at the parking area.

OPTIONS

As with most rides in the area, there are a number of ways to approach the OTB descent. It is easy to connect to this route from the TRT and the Nordic center (see Routes 5 through 9) by approaching via either Antone Meadows or the Whoop-de-doo Trail and joining this route at the top of the Wall (mile 2.9) or the Fiberboard Freeway (mile 5.1), and returning to the Nordic center via the bike path. Additionally, you can join this route from either direction on the TRT, at mile 2.9 or 5.9. Note that while there is also a trail that parallels Deer Creek from the Tevis Cup Trail down to the Truckee River, it ends in private property and therefore is not recommended.

11 BROCKWAY SUMMIT TO TAHOE CITY

SHUTTLE

Trail Type: 100% singletrack

Distance: 20.1 miles

Elevation Gain/Loss: 2800/3600 feet

High Point: 7885 feet

Ride Time: 2.5–4.5 hours

Technical Difficulty: Advanced

Fitness Intensity: Strenuous

Season: Summer–fall

Maps: Adventure Maps, Lake Tahoe Basin Trail Map, 2015 version; USGS 7.5-minute, Tahoe City, Kings Beach, Martis Peak

GPS: 39°15'30.01.31" N, -120°03'52.72" W; TRT trailhead on Fairway Dr.: 39°10'08.89" N, -120°08'55.22" W

OVERVIEW

This 20-mile stretch of the Tahoe Rim Trail (TRT) traces the high route from the top of CA 267 above Kings Beach all the way down to Tahoe City. Almost entirely singletrack, this rolling section of trail has a fair amount of climbing, some great descents, and plenty of technical challenges that will definitely keep your attention. A number of medium-sized climbs along the route bring you past Watson Lake and over Painted Rock before finishing with a long descent down Glass Mountain, with no shortage of great views along the way.

The trail crosses the Fiberboard Freeway and a number of fire roads, but following this route is relatively straightforward except for a couple of poorly marked turns near Watson Lake.

GETTING THERE

Leave your shuttle car at the Fairway Drive TRT trailhead on the western edge of Tahoe City. From the junction of CA 89 and CA 28, go west on West River Road (CA 89) for about 600 feet, and at the gas stations, turn north onto Fairway Drive. Drive 0.3 mile up the hill, past the fire station, and park in the Fairway Community Center parking lot, across the street from the TRT kiosk.

To reach the start, return to CA 28 and head northeast to Kings Beach. Turn north on CA 267 and travel for 2.7 miles to the TRT trailhead, which is just south of Brockway Summit.

MILEAGE LOG

0.0 Head west on the TRT from the parking area.

0.7 After a tough little climb, cross the Fiberboard Freeway and continue on the TRT uphill for another mile.

1.9 Reach the top of the first climb and begin a long, technical descent.

2.1 Continue straight across the Fiberboard.

3.5 Arrive at the bottom of the descent and start the second climb.

4.2 Continue straight across the Old County Fire Road Extension.

5.0 After some challenging climbing, the pitch flattens out for a bit.

5.3 Continue straight across another fire road.

5.8 Begin another climb, traveling through a couple of large meadows, which have beautiful wildflowers at the right time of year.

Riding through one of the most scenic sections of the Tahoe Rim Trail between Brockway Summit and Tahoe City, just south of Watson Lake (Oscar Havens)

6.5   Turn left to stay on the TRT. Note that this intersection has traditionally been poorly marked. (The trail going straight connects to the Fiberboard Freeway.)

6.8   Ride around the eastern shore of Watson Lake, a great spot for a midride break.

6.9   When you get to the far side of the lake, bear left after you cross the lake's outlet, Watson Creek. Continue up a small hill, pass through some short wooden posts, and take a left on the fire road to descend for 0.2 mile. These turns have traditionally not been well marked.

7.1   After riding through a large patch of gravel, take a right back onto the singletrack of the TRT; the sign is often obscured by bushes.

7.7   At the top of a short climb, where the Mount Watson Trail heads right (west), continue straight and begin the often loose and gravelly descent down the south side of Mount Watson with amazing views of the lake.

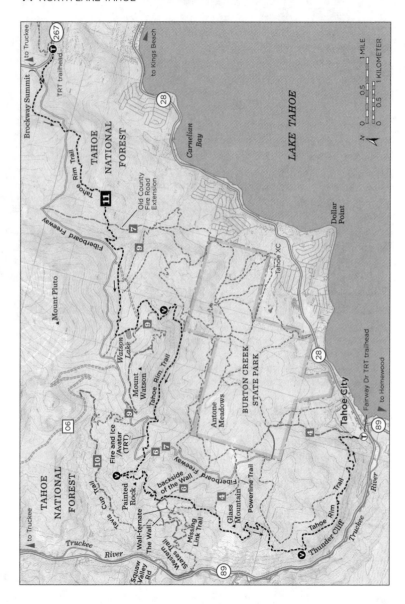

8.8 After some technical descending, the trail becomes fast until it meets an old roadbed singletrack. Turn right to stay on the TRT, contouring the south side of Mount Watson on the singletrack.

10.3 The singletrack ends in a dirt road. Turn right, then within 200 feet, take the very first left turn back onto the singletrack. If you hit the Fiberboard, you've gone too far. Local riders refer to this section as Fire and Ice/Avatar.

11.2 Ride straight across the Fiberboard and begin the climb to Painted Rock.

12.0 Enjoy the great view toward Squaw Valley and the Pacific Crest.

12.4 From the top of Painted Rock, begin a 1-mile descent to the top of the fire road known as the Wall.

13.4 Stay on the TRT and cross the fire road. (A turn to the west on the Wall leads to Western States; a turn east leads down to the Fiberboard and Antone Meadows.)

13.9 At the junction with the Missing Link Trail, stay left on the TRT.

14.3 The Powerline Trail joins the TRT from the left. Stay straight and start the last of the climbing to the top of Glass Mountain.

15.1 From the top of Glass Mountain begin a long, technical descent that will take you all the way to Tahoe City.

17.0 Enjoy a rest atop the Thunder Cliff, the unofficial halfway point of the descent, with awesome views of the Truckee River canyon.

17.6 After a short climb, the trail resumes its meandering and rocky descent toward Tahoe City.

19.4 Go straight across the dirt road.

19.6 Cross another dirt road; stay alert for hikers on this last stretch.

20.1 Round a couple of sharp switchbacks and drop down to the TRT trailhead at Fairway Dr.

OPTIONS

If you want to cut this ride short, you can drop off the TRT at mile 4.2 and head south on the Old County Fire Road Extension to the Nordic center, or drop south on the Fiberboard on the east side of Painted Rock at mile 11.2, or drop east on the backside of the Wall at mile 13.4. To add mileage, combine this ride with Mount Baldy (Route 13), Mount Watson (Route 9), the OTB Trail (Route 10), or Missing Link (Route 8).

12 SQUAW VALLEY DOWNHILL

LOOP

Trail Type: 50% singletrack, 35% pavement, 15% doubletrack
Distance: 3.8 miles
Elevation Gain/Loss: 740/740 feet
High Point: 6889 feet
Ride Time: 30 minutes–1.5 hours
Technical Difficulty: Intermediate

Fitness Intensity: Easy
Season: Summer–fall
Maps: Adventure Maps, Lake Tahoe Basin Trail Map, 2015 version; USGS 7.5-minute, Tahoe City
GPS: 39°12′14.05″ N, -120°12′4.48″ W

OVERVIEW

Known by locals as the Squaw Valley Downhill, this short loop is the best ride in Squaw Valley. A couple miles of steep climbing are handsomely rewarded with a fast, winding, and flowing descent back to the valley floor. The ride's short length makes it perfect for a quick lunch or evening lap, and it is a great way to add a little mileage to nearby routes.

This ride begins with a mellow spin on a bike path before the climbing ramps up through a posh neighborhood above the Resort at Squaw Creek. When the pavement ends, the climbing continues on a fire road up to the junction with the Western States Trail. The fast singletrack descent is well worth the climb.

GETTING THERE

From Tahoe City, travel north on CA 89 for 5 miles to the junction with Squaw Valley Road. Turn west off of CA 89 onto Squaw Valley Road then take the first left into the parking area for the soccer field.

MILEAGE LOG

0.0 Jump on the bike path on the south side of the parking area and head west, climbing gently past the soccer field and fire station. The singletrack you pass on your left is your return route.

0.3 Turn left on the bike path when you hit Squaw Creek Rd. and continue heading west.

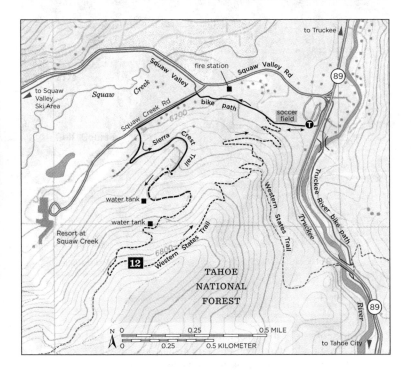

0.6 Turn left on Sierra Crest Trail, the road that leads up through the neighborhood, and begin the climb.

0.7 Turn left again to stay on Sierra Crest Trail.

1.4 At the top of the road, turn right onto a fire road just before the last house on the right. Go around the gate and continue climbing.

1.7 After you pass a water tank, the road narrows but remains loose and rocky for the duration of the climb.

2.0 Turn left on the Western States Trail; there is just a small amount of climbing left.

2.2 Arrive at the top of the climb; it's all downhill from here.

2.8 At the only fork in the trail, turn left. The Western States Trail continues right toward CA 89.

3.7 The descent ends at the bike path by the soccer field. Turn right.

3.8 Arrive back at the parking area.

Passing through slopes of thimbleberry on the lower section of the Squaw Valley Downhill

OPTIONS

This loop is relatively short, so doing a couple of laps is a great option. This loop can also be added on to other nearby rides, such as OTB (Route 10) or Missing Link (Route 8), for some additional mileage.

13 MOUNT BALDY

OUT-AND-BACK

Trail Type: 90% singletrack, 10% doubletrack
Distance: 14.3 miles
Elevation Gain/Loss: 2720/2720 feet
High Point: 9040 feet
Ride Time: 2–4 hours
Technical Difficulty: Advanced

Fitness Intensity: Strenuous
Season: Summer–fall
Maps: Adventure Maps, Lake Tahoe Basin Trail Map, 2015 version; USGS 7.5-minute, Martis Peak
GPS: 39°15′30.31″ N, -120°03′52.72″ W

OVERVIEW

Reach two of the most breathtaking scenic vistas on the north shore of Lake Tahoe on this singletrack ride on the Tahoe Rim Trail (TRT). Departing from CA 267 above Kings Beach, the trail climbs relatively steadily, interrupted by a couple of short downhill and flat sections where you can catch your breath, from the trailhead up to its high point near the Mount Rose Wilderness Boundary on Mount Baldy. Generally moderate in pitch and technical difficulty, this route does have a handful of short and steep sections, sharp switchbacks, and some very technical rock gardens that will keep you on your toes on both the ascent and the descent. There are several spots to rest and enjoy the view, so be sure to bring your camera.

This trail is pretty easy to follow with the exception of the short stretch of dirt road used to link up the upper and lower portions of singletrack near Martis Peak. Once you've taken in the view from the ride's high point at Mount Baldy, drop into one of the longest sustained descents on the entire TRT. It's easy to get going really fast here, so be sure to watch out for other trail users. There are also some relatively blind corners on this trail, so please maintain a sight-distance-appropriate speed. The mostly southern exposure along the route lends itself to melting out earlier than many other sections of the TRT, although drifts of snow may linger in higher north-facing areas near the top.

GETTING THERE

The TRT trailhead is 2.7 miles north of the junction of CA 267 with CA 28 in Kings Beach and just south of Brockway Summit. If coming from Truckee, this trailhead is 8.9 miles south of the junction of CA 267 and Interstate 80. Park on the south side of the road in the paved pullout with the TRT kiosk. The trailhead is across the road on the north side.

MILEAGE LOG

0.0   Carefully cross to the north side of CA 267, head up the fire road for 100 yards, and take a left on the singletrack next to the TRT kiosk. The trail is steepest right out of the gate; start easy and settle in.

0.6   After three switchbacks, the pitch of the trail moderates.

1.0   Continue uphill on the TRT past the trail that comes in from the right. This trail connects with other trails that drop down to Kings Beach.

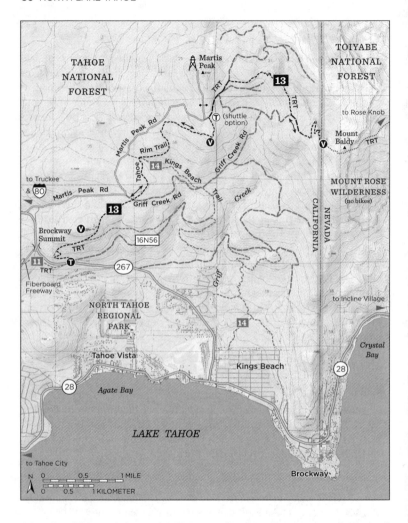

1.2 Continue straight on the TRT past the Vista Point spur trail. The trail now descends and flattens out until you cross Griff Creek Rd.

1.6 Ride straight across Griff Creek Rd. and begin a short, gravelly climb.

2.3 After a very short descent, you will stay straight on the TRT past a trail on the left that leads to Martis Peak Rd. and then another on the right just past the meadow that comes up from Kings Beach; the steady climbing begins again.

2.8 Exit the forest and then enter a large meadow of wooly mule-ears.

3.6 Begin a long and extremely technical rock garden. This presents a challenge to even the best of riders, but it is rideable in both directions. Don't be surprised if you have to walk for a short stretch.

3.7 Just beyond the technical rock garden, take a break and enjoy the view.

Negotiating a rocky switchback on the Tahoe Rim Trail below the summit of Mount Baldy

4.0 The trail intersects a dirt fire road. (This is where you would park if you shuttled up Martis Peak Rd.) Take a right and follow the dirt road for 0.5 mile, staying left at any intersections.

4.5 Turn right onto the singletrack of the TRT. Continue climbing for 1 mile.

5.5 The trail descends slightly for 0.5 mile to another dirt road.

5.9 Turn left and climb the doubletrack for 0.25 mile.

6.1 At the top of the road, continue straight onto the singletrack; a series of switchbacks bring you to the top.

7.0 Reach the rocky outcrop, which is the top of the climb and one of the finest views in all of Lake Tahoe. The Mount Rose Wilderness boundary is a short distance farther uphill. Reverse your route to return to the trailhead.

8.1 Descend the doubletrack for 0.25 mile.

8.3 Make a hard right to stay on the TRT. Be aware that this junction will sneak up on you.

9.8 Turn left on the dirt road and follow it for 0.5 mile as it dips down then climbs back up to the TRT.

10.2 Turn left on the TRT.

12.7 Ride straight across Griff Creek Rd.

13.2 Reach the Vista Point spur trail junction. The trail from here to the trailhead is a very popular short hike, so watch for hikers.

14.3 Arrive at the trailhead.

OPTIONS

A partial car shuttle shortens your ascent to Mount Baldy, making this a moderate ride, and lets you enjoy the entire descent to CA 267. To do this, leave a car at the CA 267 trailhead. In the second car, drive 1 mile north over Brockway Summit and take the first right onto Martis Peak Road. Follow the paved road until it makes a hard left at 3.2 miles, bear right onto the dirt road, and park next to the meadow and mile 4.3 (of Route 13) on the TRT. This ride can also be combined with a few trails that drop all the way down to Kings Beach (see Route 14, Kings Beach Trails).

14 KINGS BEACH TRAILS

SHUTTLE

Trail Type: 90% singletrack, 10% doubletrack
Distance: 8 miles
Elevation Gain/Loss: 400/2300 feet
High Point: 8380 feet
Ride Time: 1–2 hours
Technical Difficulty: Intermediate
Fitness Intensity: Easy

Season: Summer–fall
Maps: Adventure Maps, Lake Tahoe Basin Trail Map, 2015 version; USGS 7.5-minute, Kings Beach, Martis Peak
GPS: 39°17'1.46" N, -120°1'54.02" W; Beach parking: 39°14'16.29" N, -120°1'59.32" W

OVERVIEW

In addition to the Tahoe Rim Trail (TRT), there are a number of trails that descend the south side of Mount Baldy above the town of Kings Beach. With

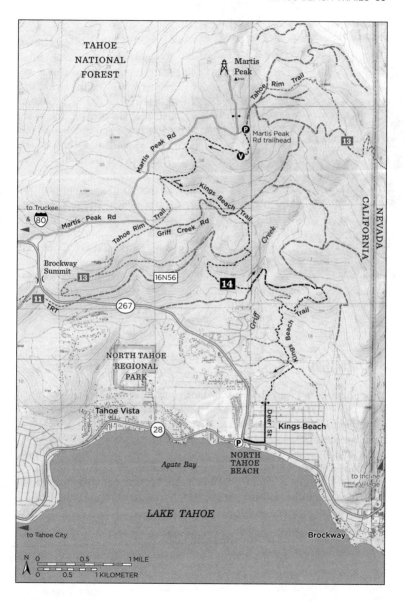

Sweeping bermed corners near the bottom of the Kings Beach Trails (Heather Benson)

only a little bit of climbing, it is possible to descend on almost 100 percent singletrack from Martis Peak to town. This route begins by descending an incredible section of the TRT that has amazing views, from the Martis Peak viewpoint down to the junction with the Kings Beach Trail. You will then follow a circuitous route down to the top of the "grid" neighborhood of Kings Beach. Despite the fact that you'll share some of these trails with motorized users, you'll find that the trails are still a great descent on a mountain bike with plenty of twists, turns, and occasional rock gardens. The lower trails of this route can be a bit of a maze; if in doubt, just go downhill toward the lake and you will eventually end up in Kings Beach.

GETTING THERE

This ride ends in Kings Beach at the north end of Lake Tahoe, and there are various free places to park your second shuttle car. I suggest the beach parking lot just west of the junction of CA 267 and CA 28, across the street from Safeway. To reach the start trailhead from Kings Beach, head north on CA 267. At 3.7 miles, just north of Brockway Summit, turn right on Martis Peak Road. (This junction is 8 miles on CA 267 from Interstate 80 in Truckee.) Follow Martis Peak Road for 3.2 miles. When the road makes a sharp left, continue straight onto the dirt road and park next to the meadow and the junction with the TRT.

MILEAGE LOG

0.0 Drop into the TRT from the parking area, heading toward Lake Tahoe and CA 267.

0.2 Reach an incredible view along the trail and the beginning of a long, technical rock garden.

1.7 Just before a meadow, at a 4x4 wooden post, take a hard left turn onto the Kings Beach Trail. In a couple hundred feet a trail branches off the TRT to the right that leads to Martis Peak Rd. If you start to climb on the TRT you have gone too far.

2.6 Continue straight across the doubletrack of Griff Creek Rd., staying on the singletrack. Motorized users occasionally ride this section of trail.

3.4 Cross the dead end of a fire road, 16N56, and continue downhill on singletrack.

4.3 The singletrack ends at a fire road; turn left and begin climbing.

4.5 Use caution as you cross the creek. There used to be a bridge here but now it is a slightly awkward scramble to get across. Continue to climb the fire road.

5.4 When you reach a three-way intersection at the top of this climb, look for the singletrack on your right. The entry to this trail isn't hidden, but isn't exactly obvious either. After a short stretch of flat trail, begin to descend a number of bermed turns.

6.3 Take a left at this intersection to continue descending.

6.7 Take another left and continue downhill.

7.0 Make the last left turn of the ride.

7.1 Turn right and continue descending.

7.6 The trail ends at a gate at the top of Deer St. Follow Deer St. downhill until you reach CA 28.

8.0 Turn right on CA 28 and follow it east through the stoplight to the beach parking lot across the street from Safeway in Kings Beach.

OPTIONS

There are numerous ways to ride the lower trails on this route, so feel free to explore; as long as you go downhill, you will make it back to town. To turn this ride into a moderate loop from Kings Beach, ride 2.7 miles up CA 267 to the TRT trailhead and climb 2.6 miles on the TRT to the junction mentioned at mile 1.7 in the mileage log above. Turn right to follow the route back to Kings Beach. You can also shuttle to the TRT trailhead on CA 267 instead of Martis Peak Road. To add some distance to the main route, ride an out-and-back up to Mount Baldy (Route 13) before beginning your descent to Kings Beach.

EAST SHORE

(INCLINE VILLAGE TO STATELINE)

In addition to having multimillion-dollar lakefront homes, an astounding number of condominium complexes, and nice town beaches, Incline Village is the closest town to some of the best riding in the basin on the east shore of the lake. While a hefty percentage of the homes in Incline Village are vacation homes, the town supports a thriving full-time population and an adventurous outdoor community and has the good fortune to be located near some of the best, most scenic trails in the region. It's just a short drive to popular rides on the Tahoe Rim Trail (TRT) at Tahoe Meadows such as the Tyrolean Downhill (Route 15), or up to Spooner Lake State Park to the start of the world-famous Flume Trail (Route 18). The trail network on the east shore has been improved significantly in recent years with new sections of trail such as Sunflower Hill and Snapdragon (see Marlette Peak, Route 17), creating new and improved loops and link-ups. This continuous improvement is thanks to the hard work and foresight of Lake Tahoe Nevada State Parks, the Tahoe Rim Trail Association, Tahoe Area Mountain Biking Association (TAMBA), and numerous volunteers.

15 TYROLEAN DOWNHILL

SHUTTLE

Trail Type: 90% singletrack, 10% doubletrack
Distance: 4.2 miles
Elevation Loss: 1600 feet
High Point: 8570 feet

Ride Time: 10–30 minutes
Technical Difficulty: Advanced
Fitness Intensity: Easy
Season: Summer–fall

Opposite: *Taking the high line to the infamous rock stairs on the Tahoe Rim Trail between Tahoe Meadows and Tunnel Creek Road*

Maps: Adventure Maps, Lake Tahoe Basin Trail Map, 2015 version; USGS 7.5-minute, Mount Rose

GPS: 39°17'53.99" N, -119°55'16.43" W; Diamond Peak parking lot: 39°15'15.80" N, -119°55'26.14" W

OVERVIEW

One of the more popular shuttle runs in the area, this 4-plus-mile descent drops 1600 vertical feet down a fast, flowing trail to the base of the Diamond Peak ski area. The trail offers a good mix of open sections, chunky rock gardens, optional manmade features, and natural rock drops. Don't be too intimidated though; riders of all abilities can and will have a good time on the Tyrolean Downhill.

A quick and easy shuttle drive brings you to the top, or you can make it a loop (see Options) and pedal up if you like to earn your descents. From the Old Mount Rose Highway, the trail starts out on an old doubletrack road for a little over a mile before the downhill begins in earnest. The upper part of the descent covers another mile as it twists and turns its way down the slope to a four-way junction with the Incline Flume Trail. Stay straight at this junction and cross the creek before cruising along a short stretch of flat trail. The lower portion of the descent starts on the ridgeline before dropping through a series of tight, technical switchbacks that take you down to a fast section that parallels the creek for the duration. A recent reroute cuts left at the bottom to prevent you from riding through private property and spits you out on Tirol Drive just above the Diamond Peak parking lot.

GETTING THERE

For the shuttle, you'll leave a car in the Diamond Peak parking area. From NV 28 on the east end of Incline Village, turn north onto Country Club Drive, then take the first right on Ski Way and follow it uphill for about a mile to the Diamond Peak ski area parking lot.

To reach the starting trailhead, from the Diamond Peak parking area, head back down Ski Way for 0.5 mile, turn right on Fairview Boulevard, and follow it uphill for 2.7 miles. Turn right on NV 431 and follow it uphill for 3.6 miles. Just past the locked gate that marks the top of the Old Mount Rose Highway, look for the small pullout on the east side of the road near Tahoe Meadows at elevation 8550 feet.

MILEAGE LOG

0.0 From the parking area, head back to the closed gate at the top of Old Mount Rose Hwy., go east through the forest, and jump on the doubletrack to head downhill. Follow the main path of the doubletrack for 1.2 miles. Don't turn down the short spur trail to the right that leads down to a pullout on the Mount Rose Hwy.

1.2 At a three-way junction, continue right onto the singletrack.

2.3 At the four-way junction with the Incline Flume, stay straight and continue downhill.

2.4 Cross the creek; a little pedaling through the flats is necessary here.

Flying off a small jump on the Tyrolean Downhill (Niall MacKenzie)

3.0 Enjoy a series of tight, technical switchbacks.

3.9 Turn left on the recently rerouted exit.

4.1 Turn left, head downhill on Tirol Dr., and coast down to the Diamond Peak parking area.

4.2 Arrive at the Diamond Peak parking area.

OPTIONS

If you are interested in making this ride a moderate loop, you can easily do so. Begin at the Diamond Peak parking area and ride south on Ski Way. Take the first right onto Fairview Boulevard and follow it 2.7 miles to the junction with the Mount Rose Highway (NV 431). Ride straight across the highway and continue past the locked gate onto the Old Mount Rose Highway. This old roadbed parallels the current Mount Rose Highway and crosses it one more time during the consistently steep pedal to the top and the beginning of the Tyrolean Downhill. This 5.3-mile climb creates a 9.5-mile loop with about 2000 vertical feet of climbing.

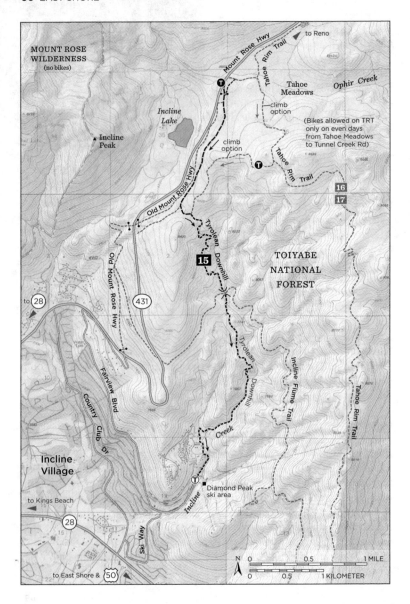

MOUNT ROSE
WILDERNESS
(no bikes)

to Reno

Tahoe Rim Trail

Mount Rose Hwy

Tahoe
Meadows

Ophir Creek

Incline
Lake

climb
option

(Bikes allowed on TRT
only on even days
from Tahoe Meadows
to Tunnel Creek Rd)

▲ Incline
Peak

climb
option

Tahoe Rim Trail

16
17

Old Mount Rose Hwy

Tyrolean Downhill

15

TOIYABE
NATIONAL
FOREST

to (28)

431

Old Mount Rose Hwy

Tyrolean Downhill

Incline Flume Trail

Tahoe Rim Trail

Fairview Blvd

Country Club Dr

Incline
Village

Incline Creek

to Kings Beach

28

Diamond Peak
ski area

Ski Way

to East Shore & 50

N   0   0.5   1 MILE
     0   0.5   1 KILOMETER

Another option is to begin on the TRT from the Mount Rose Highway parking area. Head south on the TRT and pedal up to the top of the first climb at 8813 feet. From here, a spur trail drops off the TRT to the right. Follow this singletrack trail down to the start of the singletrack portion of the Tyrolean Downhill (mile 1.2 in the mileage log). This option adds roughly 250 vertical feet of climbing and descent to the ride. Early and late in the season, when the upper part of this route may be snowbound, you can reach the lower half by coming in from the Incline Flume. You can reach the Incline Flume at its intersection with NV 431 at a pullout about 1 mile uphill from the intersection of NV 431 and Fairview Blvd.

16 MOUNT ROSE TO CHIMNEY BEACH

SHUTTLE

Trail Type: 80% singletrack, 20% doubletrack
Distance: 20.5 miles
Elevation Gain/Loss: 2440/4550 feet
High Point: 8825 feet
Ride Time: 2–4 hours
Technical Difficulty: Advanced
Fitness Intensity: Strenuous

Season: Summer–fall
Maps: Adventure Maps, Lake Tahoe Basin Trail Map, 2015 version; USGS 7.5-minute, Mount Rose, Marlette Lake
GPS: 38°18'3.59" N, -119°55'11.30" W; Chimney Beach parking lot: 39°10'3.27" N, -119°55'35.74" W

OVERVIEW

This amazing point-to-point ride along the ridge of the east shore of Lake Tahoe ends with an excellent downhill on the Chimney Beach Trail, aka the Marlette Creek Trail. Starting high off the Mount Rose Highway above Incline Village, the route follows the Tahoe Rim Trail (TRT) for 8 miles on some of the east shore's signature decomposing granite soil. This rolling section is littered with exciting, technical rock gardens, steps, and rollovers as it snakes along the ridge of the Carson Range with views of both Lake Tahoe and the Washoe Valley. After crossing Tunnel Creek Road, the trail

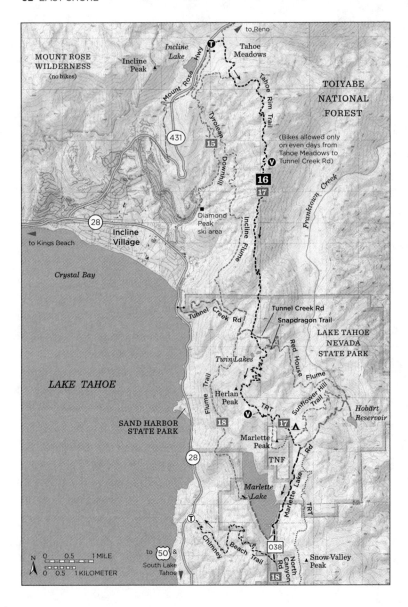

MOUNT ROSE
WILDERNESS
(no bikes)

*Incline
Lake*

Incline
Peak

Tahoe
Meadows

to Reno

TOIYABE

NATIONAL

FOREST

Mount Rose Hwy

Tahoe Rim Trail

Tyrolean

Downhill

(431)

15

(Bikes allowed only
on even days from
Tahoe Meadows to
Tunnel Creek Rd)

16
17

Franktown Creek

(28)

Incline
Village

to Kings Beach

Diamond
Peak
ski area

Incline Flume

Crystal Bay

Tunnel Creek Rd

Tunnel Creek Rd
Snapdragon Trail

LAKE TAHOE
NEVADA
STATE PARK

LAKE TAHOE

Twin Lakes

Flume Trail

Herlan
Peak

TRT

Red House

Flume

Sunflower Hill Trail

*Hobart
Reservoir*

18

V

17

SAND HARBOR
STATE PARK

Marlette
Peak

TNF

*Marlette
Lake*

Marlette Lake Rd

TRT

(28)

T

Chimney

Beach Trail

to
(50) &
South Lake
Tahoe

038

North Canyon Rd

Snow Valley
Peak

18

N

0   0.5   1 MILE

0   0.5   1 KILOMETER

then climbs steadily to the top of Marlette Peak, offering an incredible view down to Marlette Lake and Lake Tahoe. A ripping descent on single- and doubletrack brings you through a massive aspen grove down to the shores of Marlette Lake. From there, make an easy doubletrack climb to the base of the really short but steep climb to the top of the Chimney Beach descent. After catching your breath, drop into a long, fast, and sometimes sandy descent to NV 28 and the Chimney Beach parking area.

GETTING THERE

For the shuttle, leave your first car at the Chimney Beach parking lot, located on the east side of NV 28, 2.2 miles south of Sand Harbor and 5.4 miles north of the junction with US Highway 50. This small parking area has a couple of portable toilets.

To reach the start of the route from Chimney Beach, head north on NV 28 for 8 miles to the junction with Mount Rose Highway (NV 431) and turn right. Travel approximately 7 miles and park on either side of NV 431 next to Tahoe Meadows.

MILEAGE LOG

0.0 Head east through the trees along the south edge of the Tahoe Meadows to the TRT.

0.5 Turn right, uphill, at the fork, staying on the TRT.

1.3 At the top of the first climb, stay on the main trail—the most obvious one—as it begins to contour along the ridge.

4.1 After a few miles of awesome singletrack riding, stop here to take in the view down into the Washoe Valley.

5.1 A sandy saddle in the ridgeline offers views of both the lake and the valley; the top of Diamond Peak's Crystal Express chairlift is just above you to the northwest.

5.3 Arrive at the infamous stairs, a short set of downhill stairs that presents a challenge to some and is easy for others. Either way, it is a great photo op.

6.6 Begin a long, fast, and sometimes very sandy sidehill downhill. Keep your eyes peeled for two very sharp switchbacks that have a way of sneaking up on you.

8.3 Regroup at Tunnel Creek Rd. and take a break. When you're ready, continue south on the TRT.

Rolling into one of the more technical sections of the Tahoe Rim Trail on the way to Tunnel Creek Road (Oscar Havens)

9.1 After a short descent past Twin Lakes—two shallow, often dry, ponds—settle in as the trail begins a steady climb of 750 feet with a number of switchbacks toward Marlette Peak.

10.9 The trail descends briefly before kicking back up toward the top of Marlette Peak.

11.5 A short spur trail branches west up to a viewpoint at the top of Herlan Peak.

12.1 At the top of Marlette Peak, the TRT continues to the left and a spur trail branches off to the right, leading to a vista point above Marlette Lake—a great spot for a break and worth the stop. Return to the TRT and descend on a fast, twisting singletrack through wildflower meadows.

12.4 Take a hard left at this junction. You can go either way since the trails join up on the south side of Marlette Peak. Taking a left leads you around the west side of Marlette Peak with better riding, while the east side offers better views.

13.2 Stay straight on the TRT as you pass through the Marlette Peak Campground. There is a pit toilet here and water is available.

13.3 Continue straight past the top of the Sunflower Hill Trail (see Route 17) and the bottom of the trail that wraps around the east side of Marlette Peak.

13.6 Turn right onto Marlette Lake Rd. (FR 038), a doubletrack fire road. Sadly, the TRT is closed to bikes over Snow Valley Peak between here and Spooner Summit.

14.0 After a brief climb, the fire road drops down toward the lake. This section can be scary fast; watch for uphill traffic.

15.4 Turn left and head up the hill at the four-way intersection, just past the pit toilet.

16.1 At the crest of the climb, ride past the information kiosk and, as soon as the road begins to descend, take the first singletrack trail on the right. In a couple hundred feet you will ride straight across another singletrack, past a sign for the Marlette Creek Trail, and begin a steep climb.

16.5 Reach the top of the Chimney Beach Trail and begin your descent. This trail, popular with hikers, has some tight switchbacks and is occasionally quite sandy, so be aware.

20.5 Arrive at the Chimney Beach parking area.

OPTIONS

If you just want to ride the first section of the TRT, you can turn right at the junction with Tunnel Creek Road to reach Tunnel Creek Station in 3.6 miles. To shorten this ride slightly or to decrease the amount of climbing, you can go around Marlette Peak on the scenic Flume Trail (Route 18, except you will ride it from north to south). To reach the Flume Trail, turn right on Tunnel Creek Road and then in 0.3 mile, turn left onto the Flume Trail. You'll rejoin this route at mile 15.4 on the far side of Marlette Lake. For more shuttle options if you are in need, check out Flume Trail Mountain Bikes (www.flumetrailtahoe.com), which operates a bike rental, shuttle, and cafe at the bottom of Tunnel Creek Road.

17 MARLETTE PEAK

SHUTTLE

Trail Type: 80% singletrack, 20% doubletrack
Distance: 23.4 miles
Elevation Gain/Loss: 2280/5270 feet

High Point: 8825 feet
Ride Time: 2–4 hours
Technical Difficulty: Advanced
Fitness Intensity: Strenuous

Season: Summer–fall
Maps: Adventure Maps, Lake Tahoe
Basin Trail Map, 2015 version; USGS
7.5-minute, Mount Rose, Marlette Lake

GPS: 38°18'3.59" N, -119°55'11.30" W;
Tunnel Creek Cafe: 39°14'4.10" N,
-119°55'48.37" W

OVERVIEW

Here you'll find some of the best riding on the east shore of Lake Tahoe as well as a couple of recently constructed connector trails that have opened up the possibilities for new, more interesting loops in the area. Lake Tahoe Nevada State Parks has been working in cooperation with Tahoe Area Mountain Bike Association (TAMBA) in recent years to create both the Sunflower Hill Trail and the Snapdragon Trail, which link both ends of the Red House Flume Trail to the Tahoe Rim Trail (TRT) and replace the old dirt roads with singletrack connectors.

This route starts on arguably one of the best sections of the TRT—from Tahoe Meadows to Tunnel Creek Road—before taking a loop around the east side of Marlette Peak on the Snapdragon, Red House Flume, and Sunflower Hill trails. You will then climb up and over Marlette Peak and descend the TRT back to Tunnel Creek Road for the final drop to Tunnel Creek Station. Be advised that the Tahoe Rim Trail Association suggests that cyclists ride the TRT from Tahoe Meadows to Tunnel Creek Road only on even days of the week; on odd days this loop can be done from Spooner Lake State Park via North Canyon Road (see Route 18, Flume Trail).

GETTING THERE

You'll leave your first shuttle car at Tunnel Creek Station on the east end of Incline Village. It is just south of the historic Ponderosa Ranch property, at the junction of Tunnel Creek Road (FR 041) and NV 28. This is the location of the Flume Trail Mountain Bikes shuttle service (see Route 16) and a small cafe. If you are using the company's shuttle service you can park in their lot, otherwise there is ample parking on either side of NV 28.

To reach the start of the route from Tunnel Creek Station, head west on NV 28 for 3 miles to the junction with Mount Rose Highway (NV 431) and turn right. Travel approximately 7 miles and park on either side of NV 431 next to Tahoe Meadows.

Heading down Marlette Peak with Marlette Lake and Lake Tahoe below
(Niall MacKenzie)

MILEAGE LOG

0.0 Head east through the trees along the south edge of Tahoe Meadows to the TRT.

0.5 Turn right, uphill, at the fork, staying on the TRT.

1.3 At the top of the first climb, stay on the main trail—the most obvious one—as it begins to contour along the ridge.

4.1 After a few miles of awesome singletrack riding, stop here to take in the view down into the Washoe Valley.

5.1 A sandy saddle in the ridgeline offers views of both the lake and the valley, and the top of Diamond Peak's Crystal Express chairlift is just above you to the northwest.

5.3 Arrive at the infamous stairs, a short set of downhill stairs that presents a challenge to some and is easy for others. Either way, it is a great photo op.

6.6 Begin a long, fast, and sometimes very sandy sidehill downhill. Keep your eyes peeled for two very sharp switchbacks that have a way of sneaking up on you.

8.3 The TRT intersects Tunnel Creek Rd. This is a great spot to take a break and regroup. You will return to this spot later in the ride to

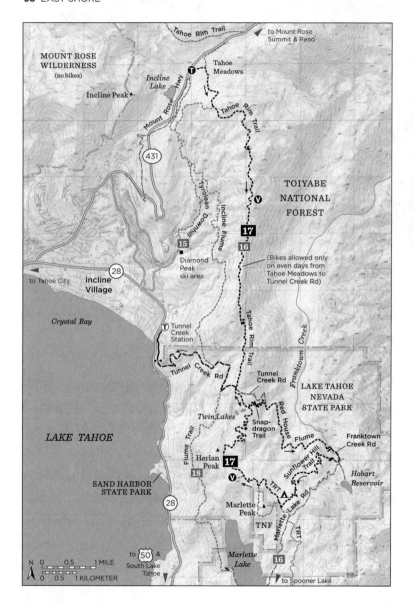

Tahoe Rim Trail

to Mount Rose
Summit & Reno

MOUNT ROSE
WILDERNESS
(no bikes)

*Incline
Lake*

Tahoe
Meadows

T

Incline Peak

Mount Rose Hwy

Tahoe Rim Trail

431

TOIYABE
NATIONAL
FOREST

Tyrolean Downhill

Incline Flume

V

15

17

Diamond
Peak
ski area

16

(Bikes allowed only
on even days from
Tahoe Meadows to
Tunnel Creek Rd)

to Tahoe City

28

Incline
Village

Tahoe Rim Trail

Crystal Bay

T

Tunnel
Creek
Station

Tunnel Creek Rd

Tunnel Creek Rd

Franktown Creek

LAKE TAHOE
NEVADA
STATE PARK

Twin Lakes

Red House

Snap-
dragon
Trail

Flume

Franktown
Creek Rd

LAKE TAHOE

Flume Trail

Herlan
Peak

17

18

V

Sunflower Hill
Trail

*Hobart
Reservoir*

SAND HARBOR
STATE PARK

TRT

Marlette Lake Rd

28

Marlette
Peak

TRT

TNF

50

to   &
South Lake
Tahoe

*Marlette
Lake*

16

to Spooner Lake

N   0   0.5   1 MILE

0   0.5   1 KILOMETER

descend Tunnel Creek Rd. to the west, but for now, continue straight on the TRT.

8.8 As you pass Twin Lakes—two shallow, often dry, ponds—look for the Snapdragon Trail on your left and turn onto it.

9.8 At the bottom of the Snapdragon singletrack take a right onto the Red House Flume. Stay on this relatively level flume trail; don't turn left down any dirt roads.

11.9 The Red House Flume ends at a small dam. Dismount and carefully walk across it. On the other side get back on your bike and follow the road, but in approximately 200 feet be sure to take the very first right turn uphill onto Franktown Creek Rd.

12.3 At a fork in the road, bear right onto Marlette Lake Rd. At the right time of year, the meadows in this area are full of incredible wildflowers or colorful aspen trees.

12.4 Turn right onto the Sunflower Hill Trail. This recently completed single-track connects the Red House Flume to the TRT near Marlette Peak, circumventing the old, steep, hot road climb.

15.2 Turn right onto the TRT. You can also go straight and wrap around the west side of Marlette Peak, which offers great views, although it is often very loose and sandy. Both trails come back together at mile 16.

15.4 Pass through the Marlette Peak Campground; there are pit toilets and water here. Begin climbing toward Marlette Peak.

16.0 Turn right at this T-junction. To the left is the top of the trail that wraps around the west side of Marlette Peak, mentioned above, that connects to the top of the Sunflower Hill Trail.

16.3 Reach the top of the climb, where a short spur trail heads south to a great spot for a break with incredible views of Marlette Lake and Lake Tahoe. To continue, head north on the TRT.

16.9 A spur trail goes off to the left here up to a viewpoint atop Herlan Peak. This is a worthy diversion if you have the time and energy. Continue straight on the TRT.

19.3 Stay straight on the TRT past the Snapdragon Trail.

19.8 Turn left onto Tunnel Creek Rd. Watch your speed as you descend.

20.2 At the junction with the Flume Trail, turn right to stay on Tunnel Creek Rd. This road descent is often loose and sandy; please control your speed and watch for uphill traffic.

20.9 Stay straight on Tunnel Creek Rd. past the junction with the Incline Flume Trail on the right.

22.7 Turn right to stay on Tunnel Creek Rd. and ride around the green gate.

23.2 The dirt road turns to pavement; continue downhill.

23.4 Finish the ride at Tunnel Creek Station.

OPTIONS

There are plenty of options on this ride. First, the loop around and over Marlette Peak can be ridden in either direction, though the route described above provides the best downhill riding, in my opinion. You can also incorporate the Flume Trail into this route by skipping the TRT section over Marlette Peak and instead dropping down to Marlette Lake and taking the Flume around. People with a lot of energy and fitness may opt out of shuttling by finishing this route with a return on the TRT from Tunnel Creek Road back to Tahoe Meadows. You can also take the Incline Flume back to NV 431 instead of dropping down Tunnel Creek Road to finish with the lower half of the Tyrolean Downhill (Route 15), if you leave your shuttle car at the Diamond Peak parking area, or you can follow the upper part of Route 15 in reverse to make this route a loop.

18 FLUME TRAIL

SHUTTLE

Trail Type: 60% doubletrack,
40% singletrack
Distance: 13.6 miles
Elevation Gain/Loss: 1200/2000 feet
High Point: 8151 feet
Ride Time: 1.5–4 hours
Technical Difficulty: Beginner
Fitness Intensity: Moderate

Season: Summer–fall
Maps: Adventure Maps, Lake Tahoe Basin Trail Map, 2015 version; USGS 7.5-minute, Marlette Lake, Glenbrook
GPS: 39°6'22.16" N -119°54'4.97" W; Tunnel Creek Station: 39°14'4.10" N, -119°55'48.37" W

OVERVIEW

In the late 1800s, the Sierra Nevada Wood and Lumber Company built wooden log flumes to transport raw lumber through the mountains on

The world-famous Flume Trail is known for its amazing, unobstructed lake views, like this one above Sand Harbor State Park. (Oscar Havens)

the east shore of Lake Tahoe. At that time, the silver mines of nearby Virginia City were booming and both wood and water came from Tahoe. Fast-forward 150 years, and while little remains of the old wooden flume, the flat bench that was cut into the steep mountainside for it has become the most iconic mountain bike trail in all of Lake Tahoe. What the Flume Trail lacks

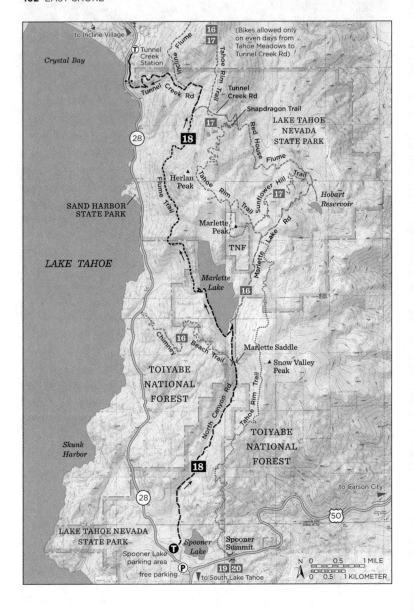

to Incline Village

Tunnel Creek Station

Crystal Bay

16
17

(Bikes allowed only on even days from Tahoe Meadows to Tunnel Creek Rd)

Incline Flume

Tahoe Rim Trail

Tunnel Creek Rd

Tunnel Creek Rd

Snapdragon Trail

17

LAKE TAHOE NEVADA STATE PARK

28

18

Red House Flume

Herlan Peak

Tahoe Rim Trail

Flume Trail

SAND HARBOR STATE PARK

Sunflower Hill Trail

17

Hobart Reservoir

Marlette Peak

LAKE TAHOE

TNF

Marlette Lake Rd

Marlette Lake

16

Chimney Beach Trail

16

Marlette Saddle

Snow Valley Peak

TOIYABE NATIONAL FOREST

North Canyon Rd

Tahoe Rim Trail

Skunk Harbor

TOIYABE NATIONAL FOREST

to Carson City

18

50

28

LAKE TAHOE NEVADA STATE PARK

Spooner Lake parking area

free parking

T

Spooner Lake

Spooner Summit

19 20

to South Lake Tahoe

N   0   0.5   1 MILE
0   0.5   1 KILOMETER

in technical challenge, it more than makes up for in exposure, with a steep drop-off toward the lake and unobstructed, jaw-dropping lake views.

Leave a car at Tunnel Creek Station or arrange a shuttle through Flume Trail Mountain Bikes (see Route 16, Mount Rose to Chimney Beach, Options), and in your second car head for Spooner Lake, where the route begins. From the lake, you'll start out on North Canyon Road, a doubletrack fire road, traversing nearly 4 miles and 1200 vertical feet through beautiful meadows, aspen groves, and conifer forests up to a saddle above Marlette Lake. Continue over the saddle and down the doubletrack to Marlette Lake before taking a left and riding around the lake's southeast shore over to the Flume Trail. The Flume Trail is 4.2 miles of virtually flat and relatively easy mountain biking, although significant exposure is a very real hazard, so be sure to stop if you want to take in the views and get off your bike to walk the short landslide sections. Those with a fear of heights may want to avoid this trail altogether. Eventually the Flume Trail intersects with Tunnel Creek Road for a fast, and often quite sandy, doubletrack descent with more incredible views back down to Tunnel Creek Station.

GETTING THERE

You'll leave your first shuttle car at Tunnel Creek Station on the east end of Incline Village. It is just south of the historic Ponderosa Ranch property, at the junction of Tunnel Creek Road (FR 041) and NV 28. This is the location of the Flume Trail Mountain Bikes shuttle service (see Route 16) and a small cafe. You can park in the cafe's parking lot if you are using the shuttle service; otherwise there is plenty of parking on either side of NV 28.

To reach the start point of the route from Tunnel Creek Station, head south on NV 28 for 10.4 miles and turn left into the parking area for Spooner Lake. There is a $10-per-day use fee to park here, or a $2-per-person fee to ride into the state park. If you want free parking, you can park in the pullout just south of the entrance to the park, immediately west of the junction of NV 28 and US Highway 50.

MILEAGE LOG

0.0   From the parking area, follow the signs to North Canyon Rd. and head north toward Marlette Lake as you begin your climb.

3.5   From here to the saddle the climb gets steeper.

4.1 Reach Marlette Saddle, which is the top of the climb at 8151 feet. Continue straight. A spur trail branches off to the left just a couple hundred feet from the top of this climb; this trail leads up to the top of the Chimney Beach descent.

4.8 As you descend to Marlette Lake, watch for others and control your speed. When you reach an intersection, turn left and ride around the southern end of the lake.

6.0 Arrive at the Marlette Lake dam and the beginning of the Flume Trail.

6.1 Continue onto the Flume Trail. The next 4 miles of scenically stunning singletrack take place on a relatively flat bench cut into the mountainside for the log and water flumes that used to be here. The trail surface is primarily of decomposing granite, which may be loose at times. There is also a steep drop-off to the west in places, so please use caution.

10.3 The Flume Trail intersects with Tunnel Creek Rd. Continue straight onto Tunnel Creek Rd. and begin the descent. Use caution as this section is often sandy and loose, and watch for other trail users and a couple of turns that will sneak up on you.

12.9 Turn right at the gate and continue along the flat doubletrack that leads to Tunnel Creek Station.

13.6 Arrive at Tunnel Creek Station.

OPTIONS

This route can be ridden as an out-and-back or in reverse. Or make it into a lollipop loop by incorporating the TRT over Marlette Peak or the Snapdragon, Red House Flume, and Sunflower Hill trails and returning to Spooner Lake via North Canyon Rd.

19 THE BENCH

OUT-AND-BACK

Trail Type: 100% singletrack
Distance: 24.2 miles
Elevation Gain/Loss: 3760/3760 feet

High Point: 8810 feet
Ride Time: 3–6 hours
Technical Difficulty: Expert

Dropping into the long descent from South Camp Peak (Niall MacKenzie)

Fitness Intensity: Very strenuous
Season: Summer–fall
Maps: Adventure Maps, Lake Tahoe
Basin Trail Map, 2015 version; USGS

7.5-minute, Glenbrook, South Lake
Tahoe
GPS: 39°6'12.69" N, -119°53'43.71" W

OVERVIEW

One of the most beautiful and challenging sections of the Tahoe Rim Trail
(TRT) spans the ridgeline between Spooner Summit and Kingsbury Grade,
two of the mountain passes on the east shore of Lake Tahoe. This 12-mile
stretch of awesome technical riding, with a significant amount of vertical
gain and loss, offers a full panoramic view of Lake Tahoe and the mountains
of the south and west shores of the lake. The Bench, the ridgetop high point
roughly in the middle of the route, has an actual log bench at its southern
end, which is a great spot to rest and enjoy the amazing views. Expert riders
will revel in this trail's technical and physical challenges along the crest of

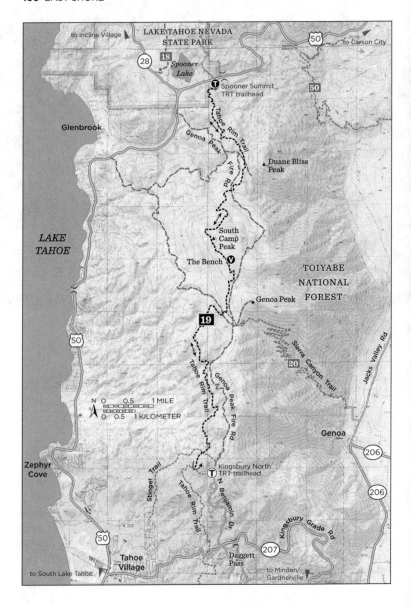

the Carson Range high above Lake Tahoe and the Washoe Valley. Bring your camera and a lot of snacks and be ready for an epic ride.

Once you're on the TRT, you'll find it is very easy to follow as it continues straight across dirt road crossings in all cases. The trail segments on either side of the Bench each have their own distinct characteristics. The Spooner side of the ride is a long and steady climb, which is a glorious downhill on the way back. The Kingsbury side of the ride consists of more rolling terrain, full of technical rock gardens as it contours along the west side of the ridge.

GETTING THERE

Spooner Summit is the high point on US Highway 50 between Lake Tahoe and Carson City, Nevada. From the intersection of US 395 and US 50 just south of Carson City, drive 9.2 miles west on US 50 to Spooner Summit. The trailhead is on the left (south) side of the road. From the junction of NV 28 and US 50 on the east shore of Lake Tahoe, the trailhead is approximately 0.8 mile west on US 50 on the right side of the road.

MILEAGE LOG

0.0 Begin on the singletrack that climbs from the south end of the parking area next to the TRT kiosk. You'll encounter steep climbing right off the bat.

2.4 After a very short descent, cross a dirt road. Stay on the singletrack here as the trail bears to the right.

3.5 After a short descent, cross another dirt road.

5.1 Power up the last bit of the climb onto the ridge of South Camp Peak. The last turn is the toughest—rocky, steep, and loose.

6.0 Arrive at the Bench at the south end of the South Camp Peak ridge. This is the midpoint of the first half of the ride and a great place to take in the view. To continue, head south on the TRT.

7.1 At the junction with the Sierra Canyon Trail, stay right on the TRT.

7.3 Cross Genoa Peak Fire Rd.

12.1 Arrive at your turnaround point—a T-junction at the south end of the trail. The Kingsbury North trailhead is 0.5 mile to the left. Turn around here and head north on the TRT to retrace your route to the trailhead.

17.0 Cross Genoa Peak Fire Rd. You have 1.3 miles of climbing until you reach the Bench.

17.2 At the junction with the Sierra Canyon Trail, stay left on the TRT.

18.4 Arrive at the Bench.
19.2 Drop in for 5 miles of almost all downhill riding back to the trailhead.
20.7 Cross a fire road, followed by a very short climb.
21.8 Cross another fire road and bear left to stay on the singletrack. Be especially aware of hiker traffic during the last couple miles of this descent; sharp switchbacks limit the sight distance.
24.2 Arrive back at the trailhead.

OPTIONS

Beginning this route from the Kingsbury North trailhead is an equally great option. To reach the trailhead, turn north off of NV 207 (Kingsbury Grade Road) onto North Benjamin Drive and follow it for 0.9 mile until the road turns into Andria Drive. Continue on Andria Drive, which changes to Genoa Peak Road, for another 0.8 mile until you reach the TRT trailhead.

Those looking to do a shorter ride may opt to just go out and back to the Bench as each side is a worthy ride in its own right. The roundtrip mileage from Spooner Summit to the Bench is 11.6 miles with 1935 feet of elevation gain and loss. This segment's ride time is 1.5 to 2.5 hours. From Kingsbury, the roundtrip to the Bench is 13 miles with an elevation gain and loss of 1500 feet and a ride time of 1.5 to 3 hours. While it involves significantly more driving, many riders opt to set up a shuttle to do the ride one way.

You can also drop down the Sierra Canyon Trail to Genoa in the Washoe Valley far below (see Route 20, Sierra Canyon). Those looking to add miles can do so on the Kingsbury end of the ride by riding the new section of TRT from the T-junction down to Kingsbury Grade then returning to the Kingsbury North trailhead via North Benjamin Drive.

20 SIERRA CANYON

SHUTTLE

Trail Type: 100% singletrack
Distance: From Spooner: 18.1 miles; From Kingsbury: 16.5 miles

Elevation Gain/Loss: From Spooner: 1680/4300 feet; From Kingsbury: 1250/4100 feet

High Point: From Spooner: 8818 feet; From Kingsbury: 8467 feet
Ride Time: 2–4 hours
Technical Difficulty: Expert
Fitness Intensity: Moderate
Season: Summer–fall
Maps: Adventure Maps, Lake Tahoe Basin Trail Map, 2015 version; USGS 7.5-minute, Glenbrook, Genoa, South Lake Tahoe
GPS: Spooner TRT trailhead: 39°6'12.69" N, -119°53'43.71" W; Kingsbury TRT trailhead: 38°59'47.10" N, -119°53'48.01" W; Genoa: 39°0'17.38" N, -119°50'44.23" W

OVERVIEW

In a descent of truly epic proportions, the 10-mile Sierra Canyon Trail drops over 3400 vertical feet from a junction with the Tahoe Rim Trail (TRT) high on the ridge all the way down to the historic Nevada town of Genoa. The Sierra Canyon Trail is a rough, wide, machine-built singletrack that links the Genoa trail system to the TRT just south of Genoa Peak in the Carson Range on Lake Tahoe's east shore. While the drop and scenery of the trail are truly amazing, be advised that the trail is very rocky and loose and has a lot, and I mean a lot, of sharp switchbacks. That being said, it is a truly novel experience to ride, so I recommend doing it at least once.

The top of the trail is about midway between the Spooner Summit and Kingsbury North TRT trailheads, so it can be approached from either side with around 6 miles of fantastic singletrack riding. From the top of the Sierra Canyon Trail, it is almost entirely downhill to Genoa, where you can enjoy a refreshing post-ride beverage at the Genoa Bar, Nevada's oldest bar. This ride requires a car shuttle, which is relatively straightforward, albeit a little long, from either starting location.

GETTING THERE

Leave your shuttle car at the endpoint in Genoa. From the Spooner Summit TRT trailhead, drive 9.9 miles west on US 50, over Spooner Summit, to the junction with US 395. Turn right (south) on US 395 and drive for 1.3 miles. Turn right on Jacks Valley Road and follow it for 8.5 miles. Park in a pullout on the left just before the intersection with Genoa Lane (NV 206). From Kingsbury, head east on Kingsbury Grade Road (NV 207) for 8 miles. Turn left on NV 206 and travel north for 5.5 miles. Continue

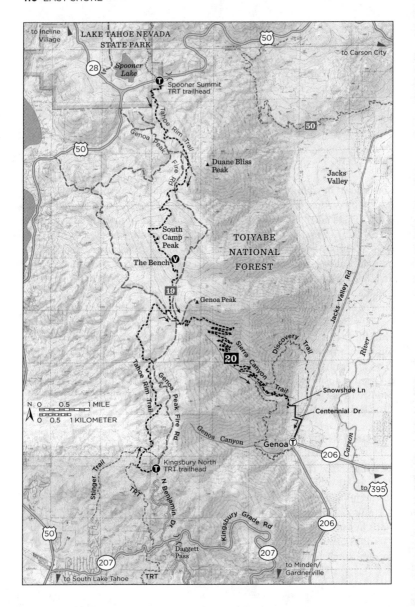

straight onto Jacks Valley Road and look for the parking pullout on the right.

To reach the start point at Spooner Summit, just follow the directions above in reverse back to US 50 and Spooner Summit. The trailhead is on the south side of the road.

To reach the Kingsbury North trailhead, follow the directions above in reverse to Kingsbury Grade Road (NV 207). Head west on NV 207 for 8.3 miles to the junction with North Benjamin Drive. Turn north on North Benjamin Drive and follow it for 1.9 miles. This stretch of road changes names to Andria Drive as it passes through a neighborhood and then Genoa Peak Road as you arrive at the trailhead. As you exit the neighborhood, look for the TRT trailhead parking and kiosk on the left.

MILEAGE LOG

SPOONER SUMMIT TO SIERRA CANYON TRAIL

0.0 Begin on the singletrack that climbs from the south end of the parking area next to the TRT kiosk. You'll encounter steep climbing right off the bat, so settle in for a long climb.

2.4 After a very short descent, cross a dirt road. Stay on the singletrack as the trail bears to the right.

3.5 After a short descent, cross another dirt road; the climbing continues.

5.1 Power up the last bit of the climb onto the ridge of South Camp Peak. The last turn is the toughest—rocky, steep, and loose. Ride south along this incredibly scenic ridgetop.

6.0 Take a break at the Bench, an actual wooden bench at the south end of the South Camp Peak ridge. It's almost entirely downhill from here.

7.1 At the well-marked junction with the Sierra Canyon Trail, turn left.

KINGSBURY NORTH TO SIERRA CANYON TRAIL

0.0 From the parking area, head west on the connector trail that leads to the TRT.

0.5 After some technical climbing, take a right at the T-junction to continue north on the TRT.

0.9 Ride straight across this OHV (off-highway vehicle) road and continue on the singletrack.

5.3 Cross Genoa Peak Fire Rd. and stay on the singletrack of the TRT.

5.5 At the well-marked junction with the Sierra Canyon Trail, turn right.

Starting the very long descent down the Sierra Canyon Trail

SIERRA CANYON TRAIL TO GENOA

0.0 From the TRT junction, head east on the narrow singletrack of the Sierra Canyon Trail. Continue straight at two junctions with fire roads.

0.4 After the second fire road crossing, a large sign marks the top of the descent. It is a very long way down from here. The trail is wide, rocky, and loose, and there are a lot of sharp switchback turns. Please control your speed and watch for other users.

8.1 At the junction with the Discovery Trail, turn hard right to temporarily join the Discovery Trail as it leads you to the lower section of the Sierra Canyon descent.

8.2 Take a sharp left turn off of the Discovery Trail and onto the lower section of the Sierra Canyon descent as it follows the path of the drainage.

10.1 The trail ends at the top of Snowshoe Ln.; continue downhill.

10.2 Turn right on Centennial Dr.

10.6 Turn right on Jacks Valley Rd. (Main St.) and continue into Genoa.

11.0 Arrive in downtown Genoa, the end of the ride. Grab yourself a cold one at Nevada's oldest bar.

OPTIONS

It is possible to climb up the Sierra Canyon Trail—trust me I've done it, but I wouldn't recommend it. If you want more mileage, you can turn right or left on the Discovery Trail and circle back to Genoa on Jacks Valley Road from either the north or south trailhead.

SOUTH LAKE TAHOE

(KINGSBURY GRADE TO LUTHER PASS)

When you think of South Lake Tahoe, you may think of the casinos that dominate the California-Nevada state line on the east end of town or the aging strip malls and motels that line US Highway 50. What is less visible is what lies behind this gritty and somewhat rough exterior—an extensive and constantly improving trail network and a robust, growing community of mountain bikers. For the purposes of this guidebook, the South Lake Tahoe area extends from Kingsbury Grade Road (NV 207) in the east, to Luther Pass in the south, and to a slight outlier at Sugar Pine Point State Park on the southwest side of Lake Tahoe. The towns of Stateline, Nevada; South Lake Tahoe, California; and Meyers, California, compose this area.

The trail network around South Lake Tahoe has undergone a transformation in recent years. The cooperative work of groups like the US Forest Service Lake Tahoe Basin Management Unit, the Tahoe Rim Trail Association, the Tahoe Area Mountain Biking Association (TAMBA), and local volunteers has ushered in a new era of mountain biking in this region. Trails like the Van Sickle Trail (Route 24), Star Lake Trail (see Routes 21 and 22), Monument Pass Trail (Route 21), the Corral Trails (Route 28), and Tahoe Mountain (Route 31) are a few examples of the forward thinking of these groups, who have provided miles of new and improved trails and have created new ways to link up and enjoy the existing trails above town. This cooperative spirit has resulted in some of the first USFS designed and constructed freeride mountain bike features in the country on the Corral Trails. More recently, the City of South Lake Tahoe, TAMBA, and South Lake Tahoe BMX partnered to create the Bijou Bike Park, South Lake Tahoe's first and only public bike park (see Appendix).

Opposite: *Entering the steep, challenging rock garden at the top of the Cold Creek Trail* (Niall MacKenzie)

While there are trails suitable for all skill levels in South Lake Tahoe, the area is better known for its expert riding. Advanced and physically fit riders will revel in the awe-inspiring potential for epic rides and massive link-ups throughout the mountains that rise above town. South Lake is home to the biggest climbs and descents that are possible in the Tahoe basin, with several climbs and descents over 3000 vertical feet. Beginner and intermediate riders, however, will take solace in the fact that there are plenty of amazing rides suitable for their ability on trails like the Corral Trails, Gun Mount Trail (Route 30), Powerline Trail (Route 27), and Tahoe Mountain.

21 MONUMENT PASS

LOOP

Trail Type: 90% singletrack, 5% pavement, 5% doubletrack
Distance: 24.9 miles
Elevation Gain/Loss: 3980/3980 feet
High Point: 9131 feet
Ride Time: 3–5 hours
Technical Difficulty: Expert

Fitness Intensity: Very strenuous
Season: Summer–fall
Maps: Adventure Maps, Lake Tahoe Basin Trail Map, 2015 version; USGS 7.5-minute, South Lake Tahoe, Minden
GPS: 38°53'44.08" N, -119°56'53.76" W

OVERVIEW

The mountains rising above South Lake Tahoe are home to many of the most epic rides in the Tahoe area, and the Monument Pass loop is one of them. This big ride takes place on almost all singletrack and highlights a couple of the more recent additions to the area trail network on the Star Lake Trail and Van Sickle Trail. After climbing the Cold Creek Trail to High Meadows you'll ascend the Star Lake Trail to the Tahoe Rim Trail (TRT) at Star Lake. From here you'll head north on the TRT, high above High Meadows and over Monument Pass before contouring around the east side of the Heavenly Ski Resort, with the Carson Valley thousands of feet below. Eventually you'll drop down the Van Sickle Trail for a scenic descent before cutting out to the Powerline Trail to connect back over to Cold Creek and the parking area. This ride is technically difficult and quite strenuous, so be prepared for a

Rolling down rock steps north of Monument Pass on the east side of the Carson Range, 4000 vertical feet above Carson Valley

challenge. Bring plenty of energy, extra snacks, a camera, and your sense of adventure and you're sure to have a blast on this ride. As with most rides in this area there are many options to shorten or lengthen this route or to bail out if necessary.

GETTING THERE

From the junction of US Highway 50 and Pioneer Trail in South Lake Tahoe, head south on Pioneer Trail for 3.8 miles. Turn left onto High Meadow Trail and follow it through the neighborhood for 0.9 mile to a gate. If the gate is closed, park here at the end of the pavement; otherwise, follow the dirt road for another 0.5 mile to the High Meadows trailhead parking area by the locked US Forest Service gate.

MILEAGE LOG

0.0 The trail leaves from the left side of the parking area, a couple hundred feet from the locked gate. Stay right at the first intersection in about 200 yards. For a quicker and less technically challenging climb

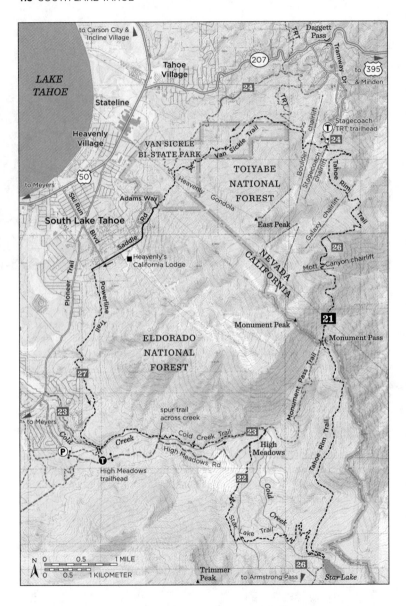

you also have the option of climbing up High Meadows Rd. (Forest Road 12N21) at this point and rejoining the route at mile 3.7.

0.1 After a very short descent, cross a bridge over Cold Creek and take a right onto the lower Cold Creek Trail. (Straight ahead is the Powerline Trail that you will ride at the end of this loop.)

0.5 Ride past a singletrack on the left and stay straight on the Cold Creek Trail.

1.2 After a couple of short, steep uphill sections, the trail levels out at an intersection with a short spur trail that crosses the creek and connects to High Meadows Rd. Continue straight and begin the upper section of the Cold Creek Trail, or turn right and cross the creek to climb the road. Either way is steep, but the road is technically much easier and quicker, while the trail is more interesting.

2.9 After some relentlessly steep riding and a couple of short hike-a-bike sections, the trail levels out.

3.2 Turn right at the top of the Cold Creek Trail, cross Cold Creek, and follow High Meadows Rd. around the western edge of High Meadows.

3.7 Turn hard left onto another doubletrack just as the High Meadows Rd. (FR 12N21) begins to drop steeply downhill. If you rode up High Meadows Rd., turn right here.

4.3 After a short climb on this sandy road, turn right onto the Star Lake Trail.

8.1 The Star Lake Trail ends at Star Lake and a junction with the TRT. This is an incredible spot for a break after the long climb. To continue, turn left (north) on the TRT for a long sidehill singletrack to Monument Pass.

11.6 Ride past the top of the new Monument Pass Trail to stay straight on the TRT. There is some very technical, rocky riding just ahead.

13.1 After a long stretch of scenic sidehill riding, pass under the Mott Canyon chairlift. Turn left and begin a steep, short climb on a dirt road.

13.4 When the dirt road flattens out, look for the TRT singletrack to continue straight ahead.

15.0 After you pass under the Galaxy chairlift, begin a very short climb.

16.4 Pass under the Stagecoach chairlift; you are just above the Stagecoach trailhead of the TRT here. Continue straight to the Van Sickle Trail.

17.0 At a very obvious fork in the trail, marked with a large wooden post, the Van Sickle Trail branches off to the left while the TRT continues to the right down to Kingsbury Grade. Begin the descent down Van Sickle.

19.3 After a technical descent, cross a creek on a recently constructed bridge.

19.7 Stay left at the bottom of the Van Sickle Trail. (A right turn here would bring you down to the Van Sickle Bi-State Park parking area.)

20.0 Take a hard left turn at this intersection and follow this trail to Saddle Rd.

20.2 The trail ends on Adams Way; follow it and then bear left onto Saddle Rd. Coast downhill, staying on Saddle Rd. past Heavenly's California Lodge, until the road ends.

21.5 When the pavement ends, continue straight onto the Powerline Trail. Follow the most obvious and heavily traveled part of this trail; numerous spur trails lead to neighborhoods or viewpoints along this stretch. Major intersections are marked with signs; stay on the Powerline Trail.

24.6 Continue straight once you return to the Cold Creek Trail. Cross the bridge and climb briefly to return to the parking area.

24.9 Arrive at the High Meadows trailhead parking area.

OPTIONS

If you're running low on time, the first part of this ride to Star Lake makes a great out-and-back (see Route 22, Cold Creek to Star Lake). For a shorter loop, you can ascend to Star Lake and head to Monument Pass at mile 11.6, then descend the new 2.5-mile Monument Pass Trail back down to High Meadows at the top of the Cold Creek Trail. You can also skip Star Lake altogether and ascend the Monument Pass Trail from High Meadows and pick up the route described above at mile 11.6. Those with very little time can also just do shuttle laps on the Van Sickle Trail (Route 24).

22 COLD CREEK TO STAR LAKE

OUT-AND-BACK

Trail Type: 90% singletrack, 10% doubletrack
Distance: 16 miles
Elevation Gain/Loss: 2540/2540 feet
High Point: 9110 feet
Ride Time: 2.5–4 hours
Technical Difficulty: Expert

Fitness Intensity: Strenuous
Season: Summer–fall
Maps: Adventure Maps, Lake Tahoe Basin Trail Map, 2015 version; USGS 7.5-minute, Freel Peak, South Lake Tahoe
GPS: 38°53'44.08" N, -119°56'53.76" W

Splashing through Cold Creek in High Meadows

OVERVIEW

A lot of excellent work has been completed recently on the trails above South Lake Tahoe and this ride features some of the best. The Cold Creek Trail has seen significant improvements in the last decade, and while it is very tough, it is a mostly rideable climb and a challenging descent. The Star Lake Trail links High Meadows to the Tahoe Rim Trail at Star Lake with 3.8 miles that are as pleasurable to climb as they are fun to descend.

This route begins by climbing the Cold Creek Trail up to High Meadows before covering a short stretch of dirt road to the Star Lake Trail. With the exception of a few tight, steep corners near the top and bottom, the Star Lake Trail is generally a nicely graded cruise as it winds its way between the lake and meadows. Nestled below the rocky face of Jobs Sister, Star Lake has a remote backcountry feel despite its proximity to town. This is an especially beautiful ride in the fall when the aspens are changing color along the Cold Creek Trail.

GETTING THERE

From the junction of US Highway 50 and Pioneer Trail in South Lake Tahoe, head south on Pioneer Trail for 3.8 miles. Turn left onto High Meadow Trail and follow it through the neighborhood for 0.9 mile to a gate. If the gate is closed, park here at the end of the pavement; otherwise, follow the dirt road

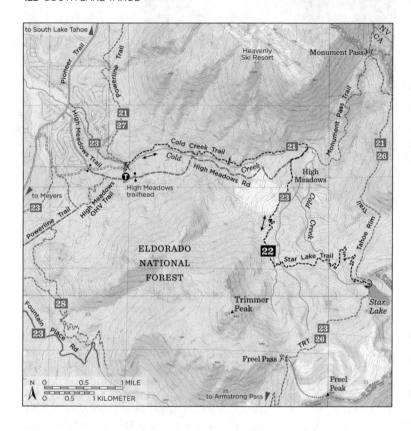

for another 0.5 mile to the High Meadows trailhead parking area by the locked US Forest Service gate.

MILEAGE LOG

0.0 The trail leaves from the left side of the parking area, a couple hundred feet from the locked gate. Stay right at the first intersection in about 200 yards.

0.1 After a very short descent, cross a bridge over Cold Creek and take a right onto the lower Cold Creek Trail.

0.5 Ride past a singletrack on the left and stay straight on the Cold Creek Trail.

1.2 After a couple of short, steep uphill sections, the trail levels out at an intersection with a short spur trail that crosses the creek and connects to High Meadows Rd. (Forest Road 12N21). Continue straight and begin the upper section of the Cold Creek Trail.

2.9 After some relentlessly steep riding and a couple of short hike-a-bike sections, the trail levels out.

3.2 Turn right at the top of the Cold Creek Trail, cross Cold Creek and follow High Meadows Rd. around the western edge of High Meadows.

3.7 Turn hard left onto another doubletrack just as the High Meadows Rd. begins to drop steeply downhill.

4.3 After a short climb on this sandy road, turn right onto the Star Lake Trail as the dirt road ends.

8.1 The Star Lake Trail ends at Star Lake and a junction with the TRT. This is an incredible spot for a break after your long climb. To begin your return route, drop in on the Star Lake Trail for one of the longest descents around.

11.8 Reach the end of the Star Lake Trail, bear left, and descend the sandy dirt road.

12.3 Turn right at the junction with High Meadows Rd.

12.8 Cross Cold Creek and take a left onto the Cold Creek Trail. (Monument Pass Trail is off to the right.)

13.0 The descent of the Cold Creek Trail begins with a very challenging rock garden.

14.7 Pass the short spur trail on the left that crosses the creek and leads to High Meadows Rd.

15.8 Turn hard left and cross the Cold Creek bridge. Go up a very short climb and stay left at the next intersection.

16.0 Return to the parking area.

OPTIONS

Climbing the upper part of the Cold Creek Trail is very challenging—even the strongest riders get off their bikes at several spots. You can climb the lower portion of Cold Creek Trail and then take the spur at mile 1.2 to get on High Meadows Road for an easier, but still very steep, climb to High Meadows. You also can skip the climb up Cold Creek Trail altogether by simply riding up High Meadows Road from the parking area.

Once at Star Lake, you can add mileage by riding either direction on the TRT to create loops of various lengths and difficulty. See Route 21, Monument Pass, for a couple of options for loops to the north and Route 23, Freel Pass, for a loop to the south. For a shorter ride, you could simply ride up and back on the Cold Creek Trail or make a loop of it by climbing High Meadows Road.

23 FREEL PASS

LOOP

Trail Type: 85% singletrack, 10% pavement, 5% doubletrack
Distance: 23.3 miles
Elevation Gain/Loss: 3740/3740 feet
High Point: 9700 feet
Ride Time: 3–6 hours
Technical Difficulty: Expert

Fitness Intensity: Very strenuous
Season: Summer–fall
Maps: Adventure Maps, Lake Tahoe Basin Trail Map, 2015 version; USGS 7.5-minute, Freel Peak, South Lake Tahoe
GPS: 38°52′20.17″ N, -119°58′56.10″ W

OVERVIEW

Discover several of South Tahoe's signature trails and ride over the highest pass that you can reach in the Tahoe area on this amazing loop. The route brings you up into the subalpine terrain of Freel Peak and Star Lake and has the most remote, big-mountain feel of any ride in the basin. Those who are up for the massive 3000-plus-foot climb will be handsomely rewarded with the longest continuous descent possible in this area. There is no lack of physical or technical challenge on this ride, so make sure you are ready for it before you commit.

Begin at the Corral parking area, heading up the paved Fountain Place Road for a 3.4-mile climb to the Armstrong Pass Trail. Continue up the beautiful singletrack to Armstrong Pass. At the Tahoe Rim Trail (TRT), turn left and descend briefly before the steep, challenging, but almost all rideable, sidehill climb to Freel Pass at 9700 feet. This 10.3-mile climb gains 3261 vertical feet from the parking area. From Freel Pass, descend east on the TRT

Topping out at Freel Pass, 9700 feet, after climbing more than 3000 vertical feet

through the often loose decomposing granite soil down to the shore of Star Lake. Turn left onto the Star Lake Trail and enjoy the flowing new singletrack all the way down to High Meadows. Ride the short section of doubletrack around High Meadows, cross Cold Creek, and drop into the Cold Creek Trail for an awesome, challenging descent all the way down to the High Meadow Trail neighborhood. Return via the Railroad Grade to the parking area.

GETTING THERE

From the junction of US Highway 50 and Pioneer Trail in South Lake Tahoe, travel south on Pioneer Trail for 7.1 miles. Turn left onto Oneidas Street and go straight through the neighborhood and through the Forest Service gate. Shortly after passing the gate, this road becomes Fountain Place Road. Follow Fountain Place Road for approximately 0.75 mile, cross Saxon Creek, and park in the Corral parking area. From the junction of US Highway 50 and Pioneer Trail in Meyers, head east on Pioneer Trail for 0.9 mile, take the fourth right onto Oneidas Street, and follow the directions above from there.

MILEAGE LOG

0.0   From the Corral parking area, start the climb up Fountain Place Rd.

2.0   Pass the upper trailhead for Corral Trails.

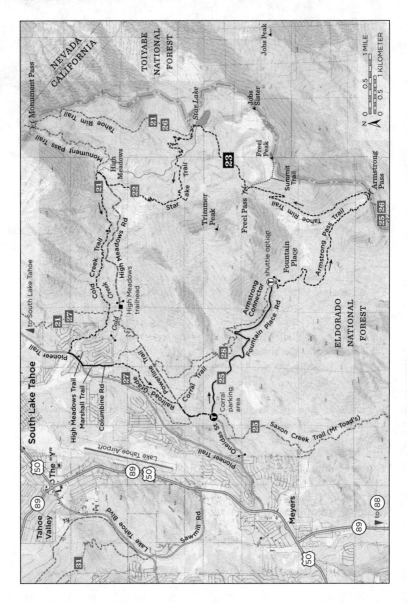

3.4   At the junction of Fountain Place Rd. and the Armstrong Connector Trail, turn right onto the Armstrong Pass Trail singletrack and begin the steady climb up to Armstrong Pass.

7.2   At Armstrong Pass, turn left on the TRT and enjoy a brief respite in the climbing. The trail soon becomes a long, steep sidehill climb with many challenging rock rolls that will make all but the strongest riders dismount and walk their bikes.

10.3   When you top out on Freel Pass, 9700 feet, you are done with the climbing. Continue on the TRT.

12.2   At Star Lake, turn left after crossing the outlet creek to descend the recently rerouted Star Lake Trail.

16.0   At the bottom of the Star Lake Trail, descend the doubletrack down to High Meadows Rd.

16.5   Turn right on High Meadows Rd.

17.1   Cross Cold Creek and take a left onto the Cold Creek Trail. This section starts out relatively flat before the technical descending begins.

18.8   About halfway down the descent, a short spur trail cuts left to High Meadows Rd. Continue straight for more excellent descent, staying on the Cold Creek Trail, which runs directly parallel to the creek. Stay alert for others on the lower parts of this trail as it is a popular section with hikers and runners.

20.0   At the junction with the Powerline Trail, continue straight to stay on the Cold Creek Trail.

21.2   The Cold Creek Trail ends at Pioneer Trail. Turn left and pedal along the road.

21.5   Take the second left onto Marshall Trail.

21.7   Take the first right onto Columbine Trail.

22.0   At the end of the pavement, continue straight onto the singletrack of the Railroad Grade.

22.5   The Railroad Grade ends at a junction with the Powerline Trail. Turn right and follow the doubletrack.

23.3   Arrive at the Corral parking area.

OPTIONS

This ride is equally good in either direction. Simply follow these directions in reverse to ride this loop clockwise. To shave off 3.4 miles of climbing at the beginning of this beast of a ride, you can shuttle up Fountain Place Road and leave a car at the end of the pavement and the top of the Armstrong Connector. You can add mileage by doing laps on the Corral Trails, or by going out and back on the TRT from Armstrong Pass or Star Lake. Note that while there is a short, steep trail from Freel Pass to Freel Peak's summit, bikes are not allowed on this section. Freel Pass is also a great out-and-back ride from either side because both sides offer equally challenging climbs rewarded with equally long and thrilling descents.

24 VAN SICKLE TRAIL

LOOP

Trail Type: 50% singletrack, 30% doubletrack, 20% pavement
Distance: 9.3 miles
Elevation Gain/Loss: 1790/1790 feet
High Point: 7815 feet
Ride Time: 1.5–2.5 hours
Technical Difficulty: Advanced

Fitness Intensity: Moderate
Season: Summer–fall
Maps: Adventure Maps, Lake Tahoe Basin Trail Map, 2015 version; USGS 7.5-minute, South Lake Tahoe
GPS: 38°57'24.04" N, -119°56'3.18" W

OVERVIEW

One of the newer trails in the region, the Van Sickle Trail connects the Tahoe Rim Trail (TRT) near the Stagecoach trailhead to Van Sickle Bi-State Park just above Heavenly Village near Stateline, Nevada. While it is quite popular to use shuttles to do the Van Sickle Trail alone (see Options), this route folds the Van Sickle Trail into a loop. You'll climb a mix of dirt and paved roads at the start, cut through the Summit Village resort of Heavenly, and link into the TRT before beginning the incredibly scenic descent on the Van Sickle.

GETTING THERE

From the intersection of US Highway 50 and Heavenly Village Way, approximately 0.5 mile south of the Nevada-California state line in South Lake Tahoe, turn east onto Heavenly Village Way. Follow this road uphill for 0.7 mile into Van Sickle Bi-State Park and park at the Van Sickle

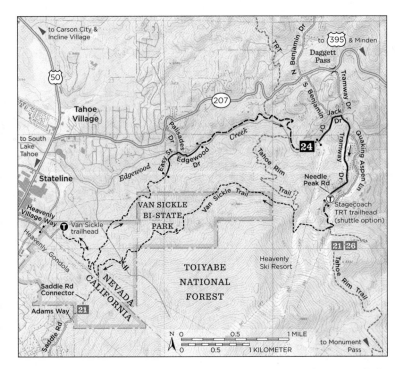

trailhead. There is a gate at the entrance of the park, which is open daily from sunrise to sunset May 1–October 31.

MILEAGE LOG

0.0 Head south from the parking area and begin climbing the Van Sickle Trail.

0.6 Take a left turn off the Van Sickle Trail at the apex of the second right-hand switchback. Follow this trail as it contours around the base of the slope.

1.8 At the end of the trail, ride around the gate onto Easy St.; continue straight.

2.1 At the intersection of Palisades Dr. and Edgewood Dr., turn right on Edgewood Dr. and continue climbing.

2.2 When the pavement ends, ride around the gate and continue climbing on the dirt road extension of Edgewood Dr.

There's no lack of amazing views as the Van Sickle Trail drops from the TRT to Van Sickle Bi-State Park near the Stateline Casinos.

3.0 As the dirt road makes a right-hand switchback, the TRT comes in from the left and joins this doubletrack road.

3.5 When the singletrack of the TRT cuts right, continue straight on the doubletrack, climbing up toward S. Benjamin Dr.

3.9 The dirt road ends at S. Benjamin Dr., ride around the gate and continue straight to the next intersection.

4.1 Turn right on Jack Dr.

4.2 Take a right on Tramway Dr. and continue climbing.

5.0 Turn right onto Needle Peak Rd. and follow it to the gate. Go around the gate and continue on the dirt service road.

5.3 Turn right on the TRT and follow it as it climbs briefly to the high point of the ride.

6.0 At the very obvious split in the trail, take a left onto the Van Sickle Trail and begin the descent. This trail features many technical rock gardens and boasts amazing views the entire way.

8.1 Cross the creek at the waterfall on a recently constructed bridge.

8.4 After a couple of very tight rock-step switchbacks, take a right at the junction with the Saddle Rd. Connector to drop back down to Van Sickle Bi-State Park.

9.3 Arrive back at the trailhead.

OPTIONS

Doing the Van Sickle Trail as a shuttle makes this a 4.4-mile, all-singletrack route, with only 400 feet of elevation gain and 1200 feet of descent. Leave one car at Van Sickle Bi-State Park. To reach the Stagecoach TRT trailhead, travel east from Tahoe Village on Kingsbury Grade Road (NV 207) for 3.1 miles to Daggett Pass. Turn south on Tramway Drive and follow it uphill for 1.3 miles. Park somewhere near Needle Peak Road and pick up the route described above at mile 5.0.

The Van Sickle also can be incorporated into a number of rides in a variety of ways. It is a great way to end any ride on the TRT that comes around the east side of Monument Peak from Monument Pass such as the Monument Pass loop (Route 21) or Big Meadow to Kingsbury South (Route 26). You can also link up with the Powerline Trail (Route 27) by turning left at mile 8.4 onto the Saddle Road Connector.

25 MR. TOAD'S WILD RIDE

LOOP

Trail Type: 80% singletrack, 15% pavement, 5% doubletrack
Distance: 19.4 miles
Elevation Gain/Loss: 3490/3490 feet
High Point: 9457 feet
Ride Time: 2.5–5 hours
Technical Difficulty: Expert

Fitness Intensity: Strenuous
Season: Summer–fall
Maps: Adventure Maps, Lake Tahoe Basin Trail Map, 2015 version; USGS 7.5-minute, Freel Peak
GPS: 38°52'20.17" N, -119°58'56.10" W

OVERVIEW

Featuring the full spectrum of riding, from steep, rocky, and technical at the top to fast, smooth, and flowing at the bottom, Mr. Toad's Wild Ride, aka the Saxon Creek Trail, is the total package. It is the most iconic trail in South Lake Tahoe, if not the entire Tahoe area, and offers some of the most fun you can find on a bike. Named after the Disneyland and Magic Kingdom theme park rides, Mr. Toad's truly takes riders on a wild ride. With its infamously long, steep, and challenging rock garden near the top, this descent will keep you on your toes as it twists, turns, and drops its way from the junction with the Tahoe Rim Trail (TRT) on the ridge down to the flats near Pioneer Trail.

Depending on your timing, and your affinity for pedaling, this ride can be done in a number of ways. The directions listed below are for a longer, cross-country-style loop that is often shortened by shuttling the 3.4 miles of pavement up Fountain Place Road to the Armstrong Pass Trail. This route then follows a beautiful, 3.8-mile singletrack climb to the TRT junction at Armstrong Pass before turning onto the TRT and following the ridgeline for 5 miles to the junction with the Saxon Creek Trail. Prepare for a wild ride and enjoy the descent all the way back to the trailhead.

You'll find additional directions in Options for doing this ride as a shuttle, starting from Luther Pass and climbing the TRT to the top of Mr. Toad's.

GETTING THERE

From the junction of US Highway 50 and Pioneer Trail in South Lake Tahoe, travel south on Pioneer Trail for 7.1 miles. Turn left onto Oneidas Street and go straight through the neighborhood and through the Forest Service gate. Shortly after passing the gate, this road becomes Fountain Place Road. Follow Fountain Place Road for approximately 0.75 mile, cross Saxon Creek, and park in the Corral parking area. From the junction of US Highway 50 and Pioneer Trail in Meyers, head east on Pioneer Trail for 0.9 mile, take the fourth right onto Oneidas Street, and follow the directions above from there.

MILEAGE LOG

0.0 From the Corral parking area, start the climb up Fountain Place Rd.

2.0 Pass the upper trailhead for Corral Trails.

3.4 At the junction of Fountain Place Rd. and the Armstrong Connector at the top of the pavement, turn right onto the Armstrong Pass Trail. This is a beautiful singletrack that rides well in both directions. The trail is generally smooth, but it is interspersed with many challenging, but rideable, rock gardens.

7.2 At the T-junction at Armstrong Pass, turn right onto the TRT and continue climbing for 2 more challenging miles.

9.3 Reach the ride's high point at nearly 9500 feet. The bulk of the climbing is finished at this point and now the trail follows the contours of the ridge with incredible views in all directions.

10.3 Arrive at a great resting spot among the boulders, with a beautiful Lake Tahoe view. From here, the trail continues to cover rolling terrain, with short ups and downs for another mile.

11.3 The descent begins in earnest, with a lot of natural rock features down to the junction with the Saxon Creek Trail (Mr. Toad's).

12.4 A 4x4 wooden signpost marks the top of the Saxon Creek Trail. The TRT continues to the left to Luther Pass (3 miles). Turn right

Trickling through the upper rock garden on Mr. Toad's Wild Ride

onto Toad's, which is immediately rocky and technical.

13.1 You'll know when you get to the meat of the upper rock garden. Some expert riders can ride this section with ease, while most end up walking. The trail continues to be challenging for some time.

14.9 Reach a distinctive and long set of wooden stairs, followed by some very rough, rock-armored trail.

15.4 A sharp, sandy left turn followed by a very short uphill mark the spot known as the "OHV turnaround." (OHV stands for "off-highway vehicle.") The trail becomes much smoother and faster shortly after this point.

17.0 After a stretch of fast, smooth, bermed riding, you'll see two short posts and arrive at a fork in the trail. Take the right fork to stay on Toad's.

17.8 After more berms and whoops, the trail spits you out onto a double-track road. Continue straight.

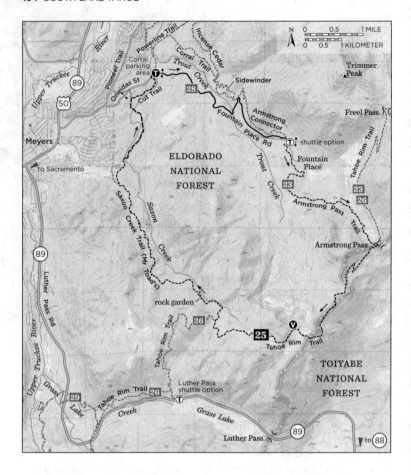

18.2 Be careful as you descend the steep, gravelly road and cross the drainage at the bottom.

18.6 As the road begins to climb, take a hard right onto the singletrack of the Cut Trail. This flat trail leads back over to Fountain Place Rd.

19.3 Turn right onto the pavement of Fountain Place Rd.

19.4 Arrive back at the parking area.

OPTIONS

To shorten the loop, you can shuttle the pavement to the top of Fountain Place Road, shaving off 3.4 miles of steep road climbing. It is easy to lap the Corral Trails (Route 28) after this loop for additional miles. Masochistic riders who enjoy long days in the saddle will often make longer loops, such as Cold Creek to Star Lake (Route 22) and over Freel Pass (Route 23), to finish on Mr. Toad's.

You can also easily do this ride as a 10-mile shuttle by starting from Luther Pass. This version has 1500 feet of elevation gain and 2600 feet of elevation loss, with a high point of 8730 feet, and will take you 1.5–3 hours. Park one vehicle at the Corral parking area. In the second vehicle, drive back out to Pioneer Trail, take a left, and continue to the stoplight at US 50 in Meyers. Turn left and follow US 50 past the agricultural inspection station, take a left on Luther Pass Road (CA 89), and drive south for 6.9 miles to the top of the hill. Look for the pullout on the north side of the road by the TRT connector (38°47'47.93" N, -119°58'27.64" W).

From the parking area, head north on the TRT connector, which offers challenging climbing right away. At 0.6 mile, turn right on the TRT and continue climbing. Be prepared to dismount and walk a few challenging uphill sections. At 2.6 miles, the trail heads downhill for a flowing ride to the top of Mr. Toad's. Turn left onto the Saxon Creek Trail (Mr. Toad's) and pick up the route at mile 12.4 above.

26 BIG MEADOW TO KINGSBURY SOUTH

SHUTTLE

Trail Type: 100% singletrack
Distance: 22 miles
Elevation Gain/Loss: 4400/4150 feet
High Point: 9700 feet
Ride Time: 3–5 hours
Technical Difficulty: Expert
Fitness Intensity: Very strenuous
Season: Summer–fall

Maps: Adventure Maps, Lake Tahoe Basin Trail Map, 2015 version; USGS 7.5-minute, Echo Lake, Freel Peak, South Lake Tahoe, Minden
GPS: 38°47'23.85" N, -120°0'0.28" W; Kingsbury South TRT trailhead: 38°57'28.53" N, -119°53'22.64" W

High above Carson Valley on the Tahoe Rim Trail

OVERVIEW

Punctuated by massive climbs, jaw-dropping scenery, and outstanding singletrack, Big Meadow to the Kingsbury South/Stagecoach trailhead on the Tahoe Rim Trail (TRT) is not to be missed. This stretch of trail traverses below the highest peaks above South Lake Tahoe and can be ridden in either direction—both are equally enjoyable.

Considering this route stays on the same trail for its entirety, it is generally very easy to follow. From the Big Meadow TRT trailhead, you'll immediately begin the first of two long, steady climbs. After about 4 miles, there is a brief respite from the climbing as you ride past the top of the Saxon Creek Trail (Mr. Toad's). The route then climbs again, up high along the ridge with excellent views in both directions, before dropping down to Armstrong Pass. Continue past the Armstrong Pass Trail and climb steadily up the long, but very scenic, sidehill to the ride's high point, 9700 feet, at Freel Pass. The trail then winds its way down through subalpine terrain to the shore of Star

Lake before contouring around to Monument Pass. After Monument Pass, the trail begins a relatively steady descent along the east side of the ridge, passing through the Heavenly Ski Resort, on its path down to the Stagecoach trailhead.

GETTING THERE

To leave a car at the Kingsbury South/Stagecoach TRT trailhead, travel north on US Highway 50 from the junction with Pioneer Trail in South Lake Tahoe. In 1.1 miles, turn right on Kingsbury Grade Road (NV 207). In 3.1 miles, turn right onto Tramway Drive and follow it for 1.3 miles. Turn right on Needle Peak Road to reach the trailhead in 0.6 mile near the base of the Stagecoach chairlift.

To reach the Big Meadow TRT trailhead and the start of the route, return to US 50, turn left, and go 1.1 miles. Turn left onto Pioneer Trail and travel 8 miles to its southern junction with US 50. Take a left onto US 50, go 0.9 mile, and turn left onto CA 89. In 5.4 miles, park at the Big Meadow TRT trailhead on the north side of the road.

MILEAGE LOG

0.0 From the Big Meadow trailhead, head northeast, climbing on the TRT.

1.8 A connector trail from Luther Pass near Grass Lake comes in from the right; continue straight and begin one of the toughest climbs on this ride.

3.8 Reach the top of the climb and begin a short descent down to the junction with Mr. Toad's.

4.2 The Saxon Creek Trail (Mr. Toad's) drops to the left; stay straight on the TRT.

6.3 Pause for a break and take in some incredible views.

7.5 At the top of the second climb, you begin a long descent to Armstrong Pass.

9.1 At Armstrong Pass, the Armstrong Pass Trail drops down to the left; continue straight on the TRT toward Freel Pass and Star Lake.

12.1 Reach the ride's high point, 9700 feet, at Freel Pass. For the next mile or so on the descent to Star Lake, the trail is often sandy and loose.

13.8 Star Lake is a pleasant spot for a break, or even a swim on a hot day. The Star Lake Trail drops off to the left just north of the lake's outlet creek. Continue straight on the TRT.

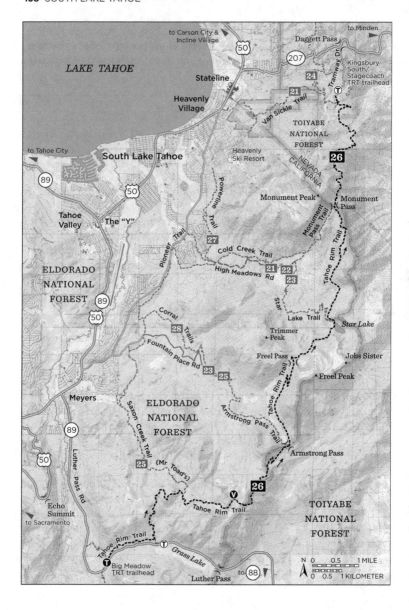

17.4 At Monument Pass, the Monument Pass Trail drops off to the left; continue straight on the TRT. Be on the lookout for some challenging switchback corners with rock steps coming up.

18.9 After crossing under the Mott Canyon chairlift, there is a short, steep climb on a dirt service road.

19.8 Pass under the Galaxy chairlift.

21.9 As you get to the Stagecoach chairlift, turn right to drop down to the Kingsbury South/Stagecoach TRT trailhead.

22.0 Arrive at the Stagecoach parking area.

OPTIONS

This ride is great in either direction, so feel free to ride from Kingsbury South/Stagecoach to Big Meadow if you feel like it. You can shave 1 mile and about 600 vertical feet of climbing at the beginning of this ride by starting from the top of Luther Pass at a connector trail that links into the TRT at mile 1.8. Along the way, you can drop off of this route on Mr. Toad's, Armstrong Pass Trail, Star Lake Trail, or the Monument Pass Trail for shorter point-to-point rides, all of which have excellent descents. To add some riding distance, and decrease the shuttle distance, you can leave your shuttle car at Van Sickle Bi-State Park and ride down the Van Sickle Trail (Route 24) just past the Kingsbury South/Stagecoach trailhead. Also, a new section of the TRT now exists between the Kingsbury South/Stagecoach trailhead and Kingsbury Grade Road (NV 207), which you can also ride for an additional 2.9 miles of descent.

27 POWERLINE TRAIL

OUT-AND-BACK

Trail Type: 100% singletrack
Distance: 6.6 miles, or more
Elevation Gain/Loss: 400/400 feet
High Point: 6626 feet
Ride Time: 30 minutes–1 hour
Technical Difficulty: Beginner

Fitness Intensity: Easy
Season: Late spring–late fall
Map: Adventure Maps, Lake Tahoe Basin Trail Map, 2015 version
GPS: 38°53'44.08" N, -119°56'53.76" W

OVERVIEW

In the mountains that rise above South Lake Tahoe, California, and Stateline, Nevada, there isn't really all that much beginner riding. Most of the routes feature massive vertical gain, big mileage, and technical challenges. The Powerline Trail, however, is a beginner-friendly ride, and a convenient connector, that sits just above town and contours the base of the west side of Monument Peak between Cold Creek and Ski Run Boulevard. While the trail is generally quite flat, it does dip and dive a few times over its course. This

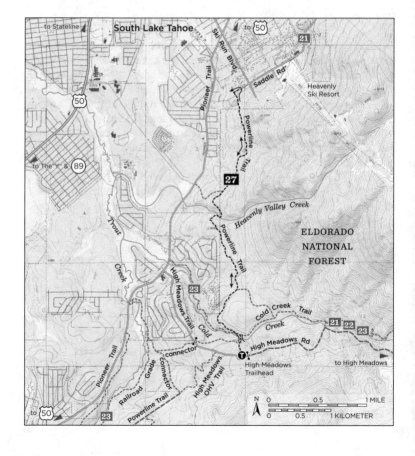

At the north end of the Powerline Trail near Saddle Road

wide and easy singletrack ride is clear of snow earlier and later in the season than most other rides in the area and can be easily linked up with nearby trails or connected to and from other rides like Cold Creek to Star Lake (Route 22), the Van Sickle Trail (Route 24), and the Corral Trails (Route 28). Numerous neighborhood trails intersect the Powerline Trail, but it is very clearly marked with signs and quite easy to follow.

GETTING THERE

From the junction of US Highway 50 and Pioneer Trail in South Lake Tahoe, head south on Pioneer Trail for 3.8 miles. Turn left onto High Meadows Trail and follow it through the neighborhood for 0.9 mile to a gate. If the gate is closed, park here at the end of the pavement; otherwise, follow the dirt road for another 0.5 mile to the High Meadows trailhead parking area by the locked US Forest Service gate.

MILEAGE LOG

0.0   The trail leaves from the left side of the parking area, a couple hundred feet from the locked gate. In about 200 yards, stay right at the first intersection.

0.2   After a very short descent, cross the bridge over Cold Creek and continue straight onto the Powerline Trail past the junction with the Cold Creek Trail.

0.9 Continue straight, following signs for the Powerline Trail at this junction.

2.1 Continue straight again, staying on the Powerline Trail. The signs make it easy to follow.

3.3 Arrive at the end of the Powerline Trail at the dead end of Saddle Rd. Turn around here and return the way you came.

6.4 Continue straight across the Cold Creek Trail, cross the Cold Creek bridge, and head up the short climb back to the parking area.

6.6 Arrive back at the High Meadows trailhead.

OPTIONS

This ride can be started from either end. There is parking at the dead end of Saddle Road at the top of Ski Run Boulevard. You can also combine this route with the Powerline Trail between Cold Creek and the Corral Trails or with the Railroad Grade to add a little more mileage.

28 CORRAL TRAILS

LOOP

Trail Type: 50% singletrack, 40% pavement; 10% doubletrack
Distance: 8.1 miles
Elevation Gain/Loss: 1390/1390 feet
High Point: 7700 feet
Ride Time: 45 minutes–2 hours
Technical Difficulty: Intermediate

Fitness Intensity: Moderate
Season: Late spring–fall
Maps: Adventure Maps, Lake Tahoe Basin Trail Map, 2015 version; USGS 7.5-minute, Freel Peak, South Lake Tahoe
GPS: 38°52'20.17" N, -119°58'56.10" W

OVERVIEW

The Corral Trail network offers a high concentration of great riding with a multitude of options for riders of all ability levels, making this one of the most popular riding areas in the South Lake Tahoe area. Thanks to recent improvements, the lower half of the Corral Trail now features a well-built tabletop jump line and a flowing series of big berms—the first freeride mountain bike features designed and constructed by the US Forest Service in the country.

The Armstrong Connector is punctuated by expansive views, big boulders, and excellent trail.

For this loop, begin on narrow, paved Fountain Place Road, which provides a relatively straightforward, albeit somewhat steep, climb to the top or an even easier shuttle drive. From the top of Fountain Place Road, you'll catch the Armstrong Connector for 1.7 miles of good turns, log rides, and a descent on the area's signature decomposing granite soil. The trail features beautiful views through massive boulders and natural rock drops and rolls and finishes with a series of bermed turns. Once you hit the Upper Corral Trail you've got 0.7 mile of winding descent through chunky rock gardens before you cruise down the Lower Corral Trail's tabletops and berms—great for beginners and experts alike. Lower Corral spits you out on the Powerline Trail doubletrack for a short pedal back to the parking area and more loops through the Corral Trails if you like.

GETTING THERE

From the junction of US Highway 50 and Pioneer Trail in South Lake Tahoe, travel south on Pioneer Trail for 7.1 miles. Turn left onto Oneidas Street and go straight through the neighborhood and through the Forest Service gate. Shortly after passing through the gate, this road becomes Fountain Place Road. Follow Fountain Place Road for approximately 0.75 mile, cross Saxon Creek, and park in the Corral parking area. From the junction of US Highway 50 and Pioneer Trail in Meyers, head east on Pioneer Trail for 0.9 mile, take the fourth right onto Oneidas Street, and follow the directions above from there.

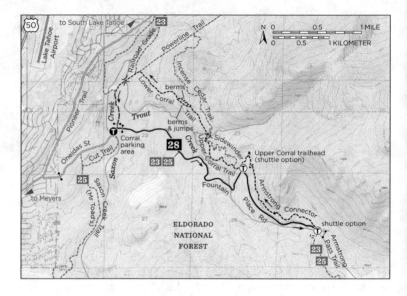

MILEAGE LOG

0.0   Turn left out of the parking area and start riding up Fountain Place Rd.

2.1   Just after crossing a cattle grate, pass the upper Corral trailhead on the left by the remnants of the old corrals. There is a parking area on the right. The bottom of the Armstrong Connector Trail exits the forest just above the Corral Trails.

3.4   Reach the end of the paved Fountain Place Rd. at the closed Forest Service gate and the junction of the Armstrong Connector and the Armstrong Pass Trail. Turn left onto the Armstrong Connector.

3.9   The Armstrong Connector starts out a bit flat with some smooth turns and log rides before descending in earnest 0.5 mile in.

5.1   After a series of bermed turns, the trail pops out onto Fountain Place Rd. just above the Upper Corral trailhead. Turn right onto the Upper Corral Trail.

5.2   At the junction with the Sidewinder Trail, go straight to stay on the Upper Corral Trail.

5.7   Reach the lower junction with the Sidewinder Trail.

6.0   Cross the creek on a bridge and reach the junction with the Incense Cedar Trail. Go straight to stay on the Lower Corral Trail.

6.3 After a short stretch of flat, pumpy whoops, you'll ride through a bunch of sketchy-looking old log rides. The Lower Corral Trail jumps begin with a small rock drop followed by four small tabletops.

6.5 The trail splits, with large berms to the right and a series of six tabletops to the left. The trails merge shortly after for more berms and tabletops.

7.4 Turn left when you hit the Powerline Trail, drop down the hill, cross the creek, and follow the doubletrack back to the parking area.

8.1 Arrive at Corral parking area, then ride some more.

OPTIONS

To shave off the ride up Fountain Place Road, you can leave a shuttle car at the Corral parking area, then drive either to the Upper Corral trailhead or to the end of Fountain Place Road. For another option, at mile 5.2, you can jump onto the 0.8-mile Sidewinder Trail, aptly named because it is packed with twists and turns. At mile 6.0, turn right to take the 1.7-mile Incense Cedar Trail, a fun trail that feels a bit like a long pump track, only with more pedaling. It ends 0.8 mile farther east on the Powerline Trail than Corral so just turn left to circle back to the parking area.

If you're looking for a shorter ride, just lap the lower stuff from the upper Corral trailhead at mile 2.1. Looking for something longer? Incorporate this network into a bigger ride on one of the nearby trails like an up-and-back on Armstrong Pass (see Route 23, Freel Pass, or Route 25, Mr. Toad's Wild Ride). Several rides share this parking area, and you can literally go as big as you want from here, so check out the map and let your imagination run wild.

29 CHRISTMAS VALLEY

LOOP

Trail Type: 75% singletrack, 25% pavement
Distance: 8.4 miles
Elevation Gain/Loss: 1560/1560 feet
High Point: 8080 feet

Ride Time: 1–2 hours
Technical Difficulty: Expert
Fitness Intensity: Strenuous
Season: Summer–fall

Maps: Adventure Maps, Lake Tahoe Basin Trail Map, 2015 version; USGS 7.5-minute, Echo Lake, Freel Peak

GPS: 38°47'44.98" N, -120°1'4.42" W

OVERVIEW

This 8.4-mile loop is by no means a gimme, as both the descent and the climb to it are as challenging as they come. Expert riders with an affinity for technical riding will revel in the trail's frequent, chunky rock gardens on both the ascent and the descent. This route also has no lack of scenic beauty as it passes by mountain meadows, along creeks, through burned forests, and around huge boulders and granite slabs.

You'll begin the Christmas Valley loop by climbing South Upper Truckee Road to the Big Meadow Tahoe Rim Trail (TRT) trailhead, then jumping on the TRT for a challenging climb to the Christmas Valley Trail intersection. Turn onto the Christmas Valley Trail and be prepared for a lot of rocks, steps, and tight turns for most of the descent back down to the trailhead.

GETTING THERE

From the junction of US Highway 50 and CA 89, known as the "Y," in South Lake Tahoe, head south on CA 89 (US 50) for 4.8 miles to Meyers. Once you pass through Meyers, turn left on CA 89 South and follow it for 2.5 miles. Turn right onto Portal Drive, then take the second left onto South Upper Truckee Road. Continue on South Upper Truckee Road for 1.4 miles and park at the Christmas Valley trailhead.

MILEAGE LOG

0.0 From the trailhead, head east on South Upper Truckee Rd.

0.9 Ride straight across CA 89 and continue on South Upper Truckee Rd. through the campground.

2.1 When you arrive at the Big Meadow trailhead, be sure to follow signs toward Big Meadow down through the parking area.

2.2 Cross CA 89 and begin to climb on the TRT. The trail immediately becomes quite steep, rocky, and technical, so expect to walk a little.

2.7 At the intersection with the Scotts Lake Trail, continue straight to Big Meadow.

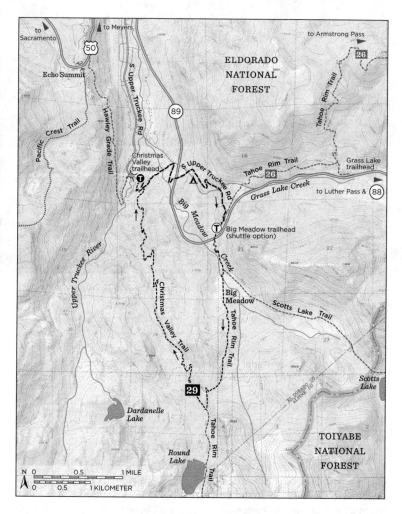

2.8 Ride across Big Meadow. This area may be very wet in spring or immediately following a rainstorm; please stay on the trail.

4.2 After a consistently tough climb, crest the ridge and drop down to the
Christmas Valley intersection.

Ripping through the charred trunks of a burned forest on the Christmas Valley Trail

4.5 At a 4x4 wooden post, turn right onto the Christmas Valley Trail. The descent starts out relatively smooth with some tight turns before becoming very rocky and technical for the duration. There are no more intersections until you get back to the trailhead.

6.0 Reach a very short but technically challenging climb in the middle of the descent.

8.4 Arrive back at the trailhead.

OPTIONS

To add distance to this ride you can ride out and back to Scotts Lake, 2.3 miles each way, from the intersection at mile 2.7, or you can ride up and back, 0.8 mile each way, to Round Lake on the TRT from the junction at mile 4.5. For a short but challenging out-and-back from the trailhead, head west across the bridge on South Upper Truckee Road and take the first left to link up with the bottom of the Hawley Grade Trail. To shave a bit of climbing off the beginning of the ride, you also can do a car shuttle to the Big Meadow TRT trailhead.

30 GUN MOUNT TRAIL

OUT-AND-BACK

Trail Type: 70% singletrack,
25% doubletrack, 5% pavement
Distance: 12 miles
Elevation Gain/Loss: 1000/1000 feet
High Point: 6730 feet
Ride Time: 1.25–2.5 hours
Technical Difficulty: Beginner

Fitness Intensity: Easy
Season: Late spring–fall
Maps: Adventure Maps, Lake Tahoe
Basin Trail Map, 2015 version; USGS
7.5-minute, Emerald Bay, Echo Lake
GPS: 38°53'18.76" N, -120°1'32.07" W

OVERVIEW

Meandering along the base of Flagpole and Echo peaks and Angora Ridge, this generally nontechnical ride primarily follows smooth singletrack that slithers through charred tree trunks, remnants of the devastating 2007 Angora Fire, to the namesake Gun Mount, an avalanche control gun, at US Highway 50 below Echo Summit. It is a relatively mellow cross-country ride that is great for beginner and intermediate riders, and even expert riders will revel in the winding singletrack and stunning views.

From the parking area at Sawmill Pond, you'll begin by climbing up Tahoe Mountain Road to Forest Mountain Drive and jumping on the singletrack that drops down to the kiosk by the gate at Mule Deer Circle. From here, follow a mix of dirt roads and singletrack—mostly singletrack—along the base of the mountains south to the Gun Mount. Turn around and retrace your route for more singletrack or return on US 50 and North Upper Truckee Road for an easier spin back. It's easy to stay on this route by always turning toward the mountains, not the neighborhood, as you go in either direction.

GETTING THERE

From the junction of US 50 and CA 89, known as the "Y," in South Lake Tahoe, head southwest on Lake Tahoe Boulevard for 2.3 miles. Turn left onto Sawmill Road, then take an immediate left into the parking area at Sawmill Pond.

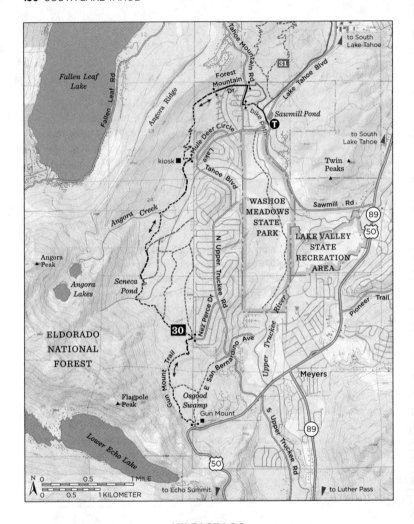

MILEAGE LOG

0.0 From the Sawmill Pond parking area, turn right onto the Sawmill Rd. bike path.

0.1 Ride straight across Lake Tahoe Blvd. and stay on the bike path.

Below Echo Peak and the Angora Ridge on the Gun Mount Trail

0.2   Turn left off the bike path onto the dirt road for a short climb to the gate at Tahoe Mountain Rd.

0.4   Turn right on Tahoe Mountain Rd. and climb.

0.6   Turn left on Forest Mountain Dr.

0.9   Ride past the gate at the end of the pavement and continue uphill on the dirt road.

1.2   Bear left onto the singletrack and enjoy the short descent.

2.1   Turn right on the fire road by the kiosk and gate near Mule Deer Circle.

2.5   The doubletrack narrows back into singletrack.

3.3   Turn right and continue on the doubletrack fire road.

3.6   Turn right onto the singletrack and skirt the western edge of Seneca Pond.

4.1   Turn right and enjoy this flowing section to the gate at Nez Perce Dr.

4.7   Turn right yet again on the fire road by the gate at Nez Perce Dr.

5.2   The trail turns back into a wide and somewhat sandy singletrack and now runs right along the steep slope at the base of Flagpole Peak. Stay right at any trail junctions.

6.0   The trail ends at a gate below the Gun Mount at US 50. Turn around and retrace your route, this time staying left at every intersection, to enjoy this trail in reverse.

7.3   Turn hard left back onto the singletrack by the gate at Nez Perce Dr.

7.9   Turn left.

8.4 Turn left off the singletrack and onto the fire road.

8.7 Stay left and back onto the singletrack.

9.5 The singletrack turns into a doubletrack fire road. Continue straight.

9.9 Turn left onto the singletrack just before the kiosk and gate by Mule Deer Circle. (You can cut out here to Lake Tahoe Blvd. for a shorter route to the parking area.)

10.8 Top out on the climb and turn right on the fire road.

11.1 Go around the gate and descend Forest Mountain Dr.

11.4 Turn right on Tahoe Mountain Rd. and descend.

11.6 Turn left and continue past the gate; bear right on the doubletrack back down to the bike path.

11.8 Turn right on the bike path.

11.9 Cross Lake Tahoe Blvd.

12.0 Return to the parking area.

OPTIONS

At any point during this ride you can cut it short by taking any of the spur trails east to the North Upper Truckee Road neighborhood and returning to the parking area on the road. You can also make this ride a loop by taking a left at the gate by the Gun Mount at mile 6.0 and riding along the east side of the Osgood Swamp for 0.9 mile to East San Bernardino Avenue. Take a left onto North Upper Truckee Road and follow it for 1.6 miles. Turn left on Lake Tahoe Boulevard and continue for 1.8 miles to Sawmill Road. Take a right and return to the parking area. This option ends up being a 10.6-mile loop. Those looking for a longer ride can also link this route up with the nearby Tahoe Mountain trail system (Route 31) or the singletrack that runs through Washoe Meadows State Park.

31 TAHOE MOUNTAIN

LOOP

Trail Type: 75% singletrack, 25% pavement
Distance: 7.8 miles

Elevation Gain/Loss: 900/900 feet
High Point: 7155 feet
Ride Time: 1–1.5 hours

Blasting around a turn through charred forest on the south side of Tahoe Mountain (Jon Rockwood)

Technical Difficulty: Intermediate
Fitness Intensity: Moderate
Season: Late spring–fall

Maps: Adventure Maps, Lake Tahoe Basin Trail Map, 2015 version; USGS 7.5-minute, Emerald Bay
GPS: 38°53'18.76" N, -120°1'32.07" W

OVERVIEW

Tahoe Mountain rises directly above the Y intersection in South Lake Tahoe, right above the Tahoe Valley neighborhood at the northeast end of the Angora Ridge. This little zone is often overshadowed by the more popular and iconic riding areas in South Lake Tahoe but offers a bunch of excellent riding very close to town. These trails wind through the charred remnants of the forests on Angora Ridge that burned during the devastating Angora Fire in 2007. Recent work by the US Forest Service has improved the trails throughout this stark landscape, and there are now several route options. With a combination of excellent riding and views of Desolation Wilderness, Lake Tahoe, South Lake, Freel Peak, and all the way down to Carson Pass, this area should not be overlooked.

This route does a counterclockwise loop starting from Sawmill Pond, following the bike path to South Tahoe High School and climbing the north side of Tahoe Mountain on the Tahoe Mountain Trail up to the very top. The route then descends the south side of Tahoe Mountain on the Angora Ridge Trail

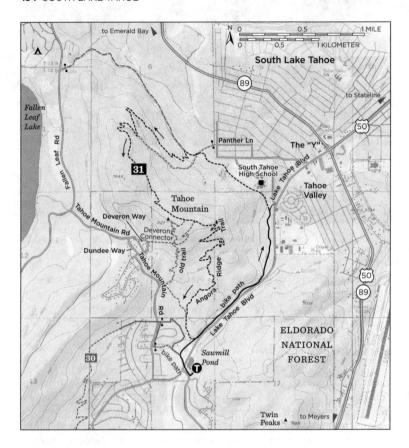

through burned forest and large decomposing granite boulders back down to the parking area. Note that these trails are equally good in either direction, so feel free to ride this loop either way.

GETTING THERE

From the junction of US Highway 50 and CA 89, known as the "Y," in South Lake Tahoe, head southwest on Lake Tahoe Boulevard for 2.3 miles. Turn left onto Sawmill Road, then take an immediate left into the parking area at Sawmill Pond.

MILEAGE LOG

0.0 From the Sawmill Pond parking area, turn right on the Sawmill Rd. bike path.

0.1 Cross Lake Tahoe Blvd. and head northeast on the bike path toward the Y intersection and South Lake Tahoe.

1.6 Bear left off the bike path onto the singletrack. This trail cuts just south of South Tahoe High School and leads over to the north side of Tahoe Mountain.

2.5 When you reach the fire road, go straight across, staying on the singletrack. A right turn on this road leads down to the gate at the end of Panther Ln. and the Tahoe Valley neighborhood.

2.6 Take a hard left turn at the first junction with singletrack. This begins the climb up the north side of Tahoe Mountain. Settle in for a very consistently pitched climb with amazing views.

4.2 Once you top out on this climb, the trail begins a rolling traverse from the north to the south side of Tahoe Mountain.

5.0 When you hit this next intersection you are basically at the top of the south side of Tahoe Mountain. Turn left. A hard right turn takes you to the actual summit.

5.1 Stay left at this intersection to begin the scenic descent of the south side of Tahoe Mountain on the Angora Ridge Trail. (A right turn here on the Deveron Connector leads to Deveron Way off of Tahoe Mountain Rd.)

7.1 At the bottom of the descent, bear right at the first junction you come to and continue descending.

7.4 Stay left here and continue descending until you reach the bike path.

7.6 When you return to the bike path, bear right.

7.7 Cross Lake Tahoe Blvd. onto Sawmill Rd.

7.8 Turn left into the Sawmill Pond parking area.

OPTIONS

From the top of Tahoe Mountain at mile 5.0, you can turn right to take a steeper, fall line option (now known as the Valley View Trail) down the south side of Tahoe Mountain to the junction at the bottom of the Angora Ridge Trail. For a shorter route, you can drive or ride up Tahoe Mountain Road to Deveron Way and then ride the Deveron Connector to reach the route at mile 5.1. I like to skip the flat riding at the bottom and ride this route in reverse up and over Tahoe Mountain, then turn around to do it again. The double up and over route is around 11 miles and 1800 vertical feet of climbing, but you get two great climbs and descents. This ride can also be combined with the Gun Mount Trail (Route 30) for some additional, mellow riding miles.

32 GENERAL CREEK

OUT-AND-BACK

Trail Type: 55% singletrack, 30% doubletrack, 15% pavement
Distance: 9.8 miles
Elevation Gain/Loss: 710/710 feet
High Point: 6914 feet
Ride Time: 1.5–3 hours
Technical Difficulty: Beginner

Fitness Intensity: Easy
Season: Late spring–fall
Maps: Adventure Maps, Lake Tahoe Basin Trail Map, 2015 version; USGS 7.5-minute, Homewood, Meeks Bay
GPS: 39°3′26.94″ N, -120°7′21.05″ W

OVERVIEW

One of the only mountain bike rides near Tahoma, California, on the west shore of Lake Tahoe, the General Creek Trail begins by following fire roads and the cross-country ski trails that were used during the 1960 Winter Olympics. The route then becomes a nice singletrack trail that climbs very gradually while paralleling General Creek. Once on the singletrack, the riding starts out easy but gets progressively more challenging the farther west you go. Rated easy on the effort scale, this ride can be made longer or more difficult (see Options).

GETTING THERE

From Tahoe City, travel 9.6 miles south on CA 89, or from the Y intersection in South Lake Tahoe, travel north on CA 89 for 17.8 miles to Ed Z'berg Sugar Pine Point State Park and look for the entrance to General Creek Campground on the west side of the highway. Park in the day-use parking area ($10 per vehicle) just next to the entrance kiosk at the campground or along CA 89 just outside the campground entrance. There are restrooms and water at the campground,

Tracing the curves of the General Creek Trail in Sugar Pine Point State Park (Heather Benson)

which also come in handy if you want to enjoy some beach time by the Ehrman Mansion after your ride.

MILEAGE LOG

0.0   From the day-use parking area, head west through the campground. It is a bit of a maze but continue to the far west end around an old wooden gate and onto North Fire Rd.

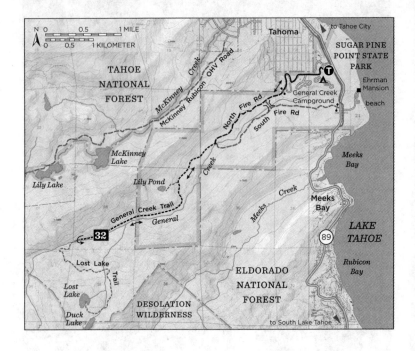

1.2   At a junction, continue straight on North Fire Rd. (The road to the left crosses General Creek and connects to South Fire Rd.)

2.1   At the west end of the fire roads, continue west onto the singletrack of the General Creek Trail.

2.9   The Lily Pond Trail climbs steeply to the right at this junction. Stay left on the General Creek Trail.

4.3   The trail begins to steepen significantly; several short hike-a-bike sections await those continuing farther. This is a good spot for beginners or anyone with an aversion to technical riding to turn around.

4.9   The trail crosses General Creek. I recommend turning around here.

6.9   From the turnaround, continue past the Lily Pond Trail.

7.7   Turn left back onto North Fire Rd. (You could go either way here but North Fire Rd. is less sandy.)

8.6   Continue straight on North Fire Rd. (If you took South Fire Rd., you could cross back over here.)

9.0   North Fire Rd. ends at the west end of the campground; continue east
through the campground.

9.8   Arrive at the day-use parking area.

OPTIONS

Those looking for a very easy ride may want to consider a simple loop of the
North and South fire roads. If you have energy to spare at the top of the General
Creek Trail you can ride up to Lost Lake on a loose and wide old doubletrack;
this adds almost 5 miles and 900 vertical feet to the ride, but be warned that
you will be pushing or carrying your bike for part of the way. At the end of the
ride you can also exit via South Fire Road and return to the campground via
the bike path.

TRUCKEE

Just 15 miles north of Lake Tahoe, Truckee, California, is an easy-to-access recreational paradise. Interstate 80 runs right through the middle of town, making it very simple to get to and from this mountain playground. This historic town has grown significantly over the past several decades and boasts a population of over sixteen thousand residents according to the 2013 census. Recreational opportunities abound, with mountain biking, hiking, rock climbing, and water and winter sports attracting a vibrant community of local and visiting outdoor enthusiasts.

Truckee features a wealth of great riding near town and lies in close proximity to Donner Summit and North Lake Tahoe. Recent and ongoing trail construction in the area on the Donner Lake Rim Trail (Route 35) and throughout Tahoe Donner is adding to the already impressive mountain biking opportunities, which only promise to get better as time goes on. Truckee is also home to several low-elevation rides that are often the first to melt out in spring and the last to get covered with snow in the winter. A new and exciting addition to the bike scene is Truckee Bike Park (see Appendix), which is free to the public and offers a pump track, dirt jumps, flow lines, and a drop zone—all of which are designed with safety and skills progression in mind. Northstar offers lift-served downhill mountain biking, bike rentals, and lessons (see Appendix). No matter what kind of riding you're into, the trails and bike parks around Truckee have got you covered.

Opposite: *Leaning it over on the Hidden Gem Trail on Tahoe Donner's Euer Valley Loop* (Heather Benson)

33 JACKASS RIDGE

LOOP

Trail Type: 60% singletrack, 40% doubletrack
Distance: 4.1 miles
Elevation Gain/Loss: 600/600 feet
High Point: 6438 feet
Ride Time: 30 minutes–1 hour
Technical Difficulty: Intermediate

Fitness Intensity: Easy
Season: Late spring–fall
Maps: Adventure Maps, Lake Tahoe Basin Trail Map, 2015 version; USGS 7.5-minute, Truckee
GPS: 39°18'33.77" N, -120°12'23.35" W

OVERVIEW

In addition to having a funny name, the Jackass Ridge loop is a really great, short ride close to downtown Truckee. Situated on the east end of the ridge that makes up the south wall of Coldstream Canyon, this 4.1-mile ride features 2.5 miles of singletrack that has seen some major improvements in the past couple of years. A number of natural rock features and well-built berms will have you finishing this ride with a smile on your face and possibly heading back for another round. With a short length and minimal vertical gain, it's a perfect quick lap for beginner and intermediate riders, yet the well-made berms and optional rock features will keep experts interested all the way to the end.

GETTING THERE

From the western junction of Interstate 80 and CA 89 in Truckee, travel 1 mile south on CA 89 to an unsigned dirt road on the right. (It is 0.4 mile south of the junction of West River Street and CA 89.) Go approximately 200 feet on the dirt road and park in the small dirt parking area by the green Forest Service gate. Space is limited here, but there is plenty of parking in the large pullout on the west side of CA 89 just north of this road.

MILEAGE LOG

0.0 Head west, uphill, on the fire road past the gate.

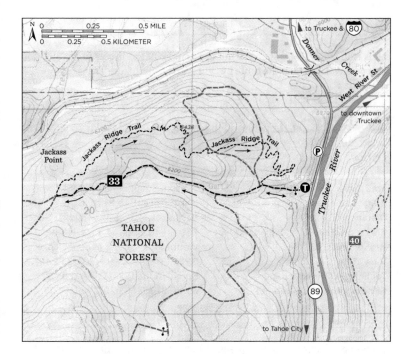

0.2 Stay on the road, and as it begins to bear left, you will see the end of the Jackass Ridge singletrack coming in on the right; this is where you will end the loop.

0.3 Continue straight past a dirt road on the right.

0.5 As the main fire road makes a sweeping left turn, continue straight onto the narrower and less-traveled doubletrack. Stay on this road to the next junction.

1.4 At this four-way junction, turn right onto the singletrack that is the Jackass Ridge Trail. The next mile or so is rolling terrain and a gentle uphill.

2.4 This is the ride's highest point, and the next 1.5 miles are almost entirely downhill.

3.9 The singletrack ends at the fire road that you pedaled up earlier. Turn left to return to the parking area.

4.1 Arrive at the parking area.

OPTIONS

This ride is relatively short, so doing a couple of laps is certainly an option. You can also lengthen the route by riding to the start from Truckee.

34 HOLE IN THE GROUND

LOOP

Trail Type: 70% singletrack, 20% doubletrack, 10% pavement
Distance: 15.8 miles
Elevation Gain/Loss: 2210/2210 feet
High Point: 8022 feet
Ride Time: 2–4 hours
Technical Difficulty: Expert
Fitness Intensity: Moderate

Season: Summer–fall
Maps: Adventure Maps, Lake Tahoe Basin Trail Map, 2015 version; USGS 7.5-minute, Soda Springs, Norden, Webber Peak, Independence Lake
GPS: 39°19'41.02" N, -120°23'22.48" W; Boreal Ridge Road parking area: 39°20'27.35" N, -120°20'51.38" W

OVERVIEW

A classic Truckee area ride perched high atop Donner Summit, this 15.8-mile loop traverses the rugged and scenic terrain just north of Interstate 80 and west of Castle Peak. Riders who enjoy a technical challenge will revel in this trail's frequent, chunky rock gardens and the summit's signature large granite slabs. The majestic views of Castle Peak's summit ridgeline and the remote backcountry feel of the trail alone make a ride on the Hole in the Ground loop worth the trip. This trail's higher elevation means it is one of the last to melt out in the spring, sometimes not until mid-July, and one of the first to get snowed in come fall, so be sure to check with local shops for current conditions.

This route starts just off of I-80 at the Lola Montez Lakes trailhead and follows a mix of paved and dirt roads up to Castle Valley and the beginning of the Hole in the Ground (HITG) Trail. You'll then climb up onto Andesite Ridge, with impressive views of Castle Peak, before following a circuitous and technically challenging route to Lower Lola Montez Lake. After that the route becomes a mix of fire road and singletrack back to the trailhead.

Descending Andesite Ridge on the Hole in the Ground Trail near Castle Peak

GETTING THERE

From the western junction of I-80 and CA 89 in Truckee, travel 11 miles west on I-80 to the Soda Springs (Norden) exit. At the bottom of the ramp, turn right onto Donner Pass Road and take an immediate right onto Sherrit Lane. Drive 0.3 mile, past the fire station and up the hill, and park near the Lola Montez Lakes trailhead sign.

MILEAGE LOG

0.0 Head west, back down Sherrit Ln.

0.3 Turn left on Donner Pass Rd., cross over I-80, and ride through Soda Springs.

1.7 Turn left onto the dirt road with the sign for the Central Sierra Snow Laboratory. It's the last turn before a long, uphill straightaway on the road. Follow the main path of this road—don't make any turns—past a few homes and the laboratory, and then parallel the highway until you reach the Boreal Mountain Resort parking lot.

3.0 Ride east, straight across the parking lot.

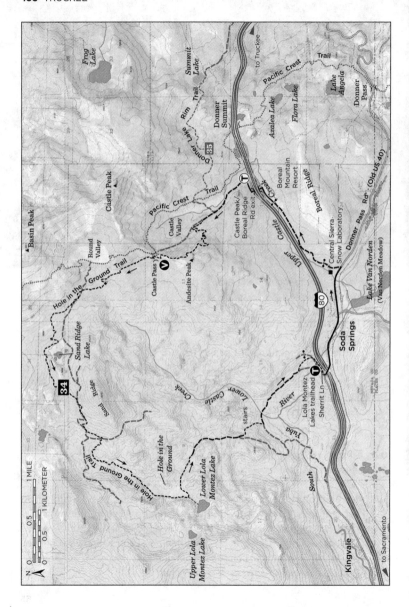

3.2 Turn left, cross underneath I-80, then follow the road uphill to the right.

3.5 At the end of the pavement, continue straight onto the main dirt road and follow it as it climbs and contours along the west side of Castle Valley; don't turn off it until you've reached the Hole in the Ground Trail.

4.5 A dirt pullout and sign on the left mark the beginning of the Hole in the Ground singletrack. Turn left onto the trail and begin the climb toward Andesite Peak.

5.7 Reach the top of the climb and the highest point of the ride. Enjoy an awesome view of Castle Peak's southwest side before you begin the descent.

7.6 A spur trail cuts off to the right up to Round Valley and the PCT. Stay on the Hole in the Ground Trail.

8.7 Pass a spur trail to Sand Ridge Lake.

12.6 At the junction with the spur trail to Lower Lola Montez Lake, go right to take a break at the lake—a great spot to eat lunch or take a dip. Otherwise, veer left to stay on the Hole in the Ground Trail.

13.0 The singletrack turns into a gravelly fire road. Follow the main path of this fire road downhill; don't make any turns until you see a sign for the trail on the left.

14.2 Take a hard left off of the fire road onto the singletrack by the sign. This section is very steep, challenging, loose, and dusty and is littered with rocks and wooden steps. Be careful.

14.7 Take a hard left back onto the gravelly fire road.

15.0 Cross Lower Castle Creek. This creek is often quite deep, so keeping your feet dry is a challenge. Begin the final climb back to the trailhead.

15.6 Turn left off the dirt road and back onto singletrack by the sign, and begin a punchy little climb back to the trailhead.

15.8 Arrive back at the Lola Montez Lakes trailhead.

OPTIONS

With two vehicles you can shuttle the first 3.5 miles of this ride by leaving one at the Lola Montez Lakes trailhead and driving 2.5 miles east on I-80 to the Castle Peak/Boreal Ridge Road exit. Head north off the exit, drive under the freeway and up the hill, and park where the pavement ends. Pick up the directions for this route at mile 3.5. This loop can be added on to the Donner Lake Rim Trail (Route 35) for those looking for a huge day in the saddle.

35 DONNER LAKE RIM TRAIL

OUT-AND-BACK

Trail Type: 80% singletrack, 20% doubletrack
Distance: 15.6 miles
Elevation Gain/Loss: 2000/2000 feet
High Point: 7650 feet
Ride Time: 2–4 hours

Technical Difficulty: Advanced
Fitness Intensity: Strenuous
Season: Summer–fall
Maps: Adventure Maps, Lake Tahoe Basin Trail Map, 2015 version; USGS 7.5-minute, Norden
GPS: 39°20'40.24" N, -120°16'20.47" W

OVERVIEW

When completed, the Donner Lake Rim Trail (DLRT) will be a 23-mile stretch of trail that circles the rim of the Donner Lake basin. Currently, the DLRT is 8 miles of trail that travels from Glacier Way in Tahoe Donner to the Castle Valley on Donner Summit. Over its course, the trail features a great variety of terrain, from fast, flowing singletrack to technical switchbacks and some of Donner Summit's signature boulders and slab rock. The DLRT can be ridden in a number of ways—as a shuttle ride from either end, as an out-and-back (described here), or as a connector from Truckee up to the Hole in the Ground Trail (Route 34).

From the trailhead on Glacier Way, you'll begin with a mellow but very scenic climb above Donner Lake to the Drifter Hut above Negro Canyon. From the Drifter Hut the route drops steeply down 1.4 miles of sidehill trail with a number of sharp switchbacks to the floor of Negro Canyon. The route then climbs gradually west out of Negro Canyon, eventually becoming a doubletrack fire road, up to Summit Lake. After Summit Lake, the trail turns back into singletrack that contours around the south face of Castle Peak with plenty of technical challenges to keep you on your toes. When the trail ends at a dirt road in Castle Valley, turn around and retrace your route back to the trailhead.

GETTING THERE

From the western junction of Interstate 80 and CA 89 in Truckee, go north on CA 89 for 800 feet to its end at Donner Pass Road. Turn left on Donner Pass Road and go 0.6 mile to Northwoods Boulevard. Turn right on Northwoods Boulevard and

Technical challenges abound on the Donner Lake Rim Trail between Summit Lake and Castle Valley.

go 1.4 miles. From here, the boulevard forms a loop; turn left and go 2.4 miles. Turn left on Davos Drive (this will be the third intersection with Davos Drive), then take the next right on Skislope Way and follow it uphill for 2.2 miles to Glacier Way. Turn left on Glacier Way and park by the DLRT trailhead.

MILEAGE LOG

0.0 From the trailhead, go west on the DLRT, which is a doubletrack road until you reach the Negro Canyon Overlook.

0.9 Pass the Negro Canyon overlook.

1.7 Reach the top of the first climb, just above the Drifter Hut, a small warming hut for the Tahoe Donner Cross Country Ski Area.

1.9 After a short descent, turn left and begin the Negro Canyon descent. Beware of the many sharp switchbacks that will sneak up on you.

3.3 At the bottom of the descent, take a right, following the signs for the DLRT and Summit Lake. The Wendin Way Access Trail comes up from the left.

3.5 Turn right off the short section of downhill doubletrack and begin a beautiful sidehill climb.

4.7 The singletrack turns into a doubletrack road; continue to follow it uphill until you reach Summit Lake. (This section may be rerouted on singletrack in the near future.)

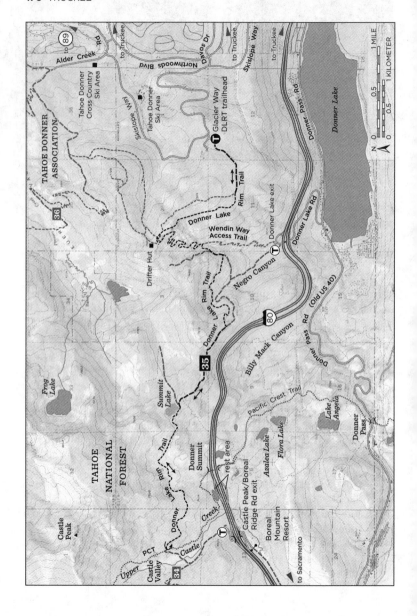

5.8   Summit Lake is a nice spot for a break. The trail becomes a more technically difficult singletrack again beyond this point.

7.2   Enjoy some challenging rock slabs and gardens for approximately the next 0.5 mile along the south side of Castle Peak.

7.8   The singletrack ends at a dirt road in the Castle Valley near the Pacific Crest Trail. Turn around here.

9.8   Arrive back at Summit Lake. The trail turns to doubletrack; follow it east.

11.0   The doubletrack turns back into singletrack; begin a great sidehill descent back into Negro Canyon.

12.1   Turn left on the doubletrack, climb briefly, and then turn right to continue on singletrack. Follow signs for the DLRT.

12.4   Turn left and begin the climb back up the switchbacks toward the Drifter Hut.

13.8   At what seems like the top of the climb, turn right and climb just a little more before descending back to the trailhead at Glacier Way.

15.6   Arrive at the trailhead on Glacier Way.

OPTIONS

Hardcore riders will often use the DLRT to access the Hole in the Ground (HITG) Trail and do a massive lollipop loop, or you can just do an out-and-back on the first climb of the Andesite Ridge. If you want to continue on to the HITG Trail from mile 7.8 above, turn left and descend the road for 0.6 mile, cross Castle Creek, and turn right to get to the HITG Trail. If you aren't that hardcore, you can also shuttle yourself up to Donner Summit and ride the DLRT Trail one way from there. From the Glacier Way trailhead, just return to I-80 and go west for approximately 7 miles to the Castle Peak and Boreal Ridge Road exit. Head north off the exit, drive under the freeway and up the hill, and park where the pavement ends. Ride north on the dirt road for 0.6 mile, take the first right, and climb another 0.6 mile to the junction with the DLRT.

   You can also start this ride from Negro Canyon by riding 1 mile up what is called the Wendin Way Access Trail to the DLRT, joining the route at mile 3.3 above. From Truckee, go 5.4 miles west on I-80 to the Donner Lake exit and pull into a dirt road that leaves the interchange on the north side of I-80 and quickly becomes a large dirt parking area on the right. The Wendin Way Access Trail leaves the parking area just next to the trailhead kiosk.

36 EUER VALLEY

LOOP

Trail Type: 50% singletrack, 50% doubletrack
Distance: 8.6 miles
Elevation Gain/Loss: 980/980 feet
High Point: 7122 feet
Ride Time: 1–2 hours
Technical Difficulty: Intermediate

Fitness Intensity: Easy
Season: Summer–fall
Maps: Adventure Maps, Lake Tahoe Basin Trail Map, 2015 version; USGS 7.5-minute, Norden, Independence Lake, Truckee
GPS: 39°10′22.17″ N, 20°15′15.47″ W

OVERVIEW

The extensive network of multiuse trails and dirt roads that crisscross the Tahoe Donner Cross Country Ski Area during the summer months have been significantly improved for mountain bikers in recent years. Here you'll find several purpose-built mountain biking trails and this loop of Euer Valley highlights some of the best of them on a mix of singletrack and fire roads that offer excellent scenery along the way. There is also minimal climbing, making this ride excellent for beginner and intermediate riders while still exciting enough for experts. The ski area offers bike rentals at the lodge on Alder Creek Road.

The route starts with a casual climb on the dirt roads of the ski area before dropping into a twisting descent down the Motherlode and Hidden Gem trails into the Euer Valley. After crossing the Euer Valley you will parallel it on a new singletrack that loops you back along its north side for a short climb up the Cinnamon Twist Trail to finish the loop. This route is great on its own but can be easily incorporated with other nearby trails to create a longer route or all-day epic tour.

GETTING THERE

From the western junction of Interstate 80 and CA 89 in Truckee, go north on CA 89 for 800 feet to its end at Donner Pass Road. Turn left on Donner Pass Road and go 0.6 mile to Northwoods Boulevard. Turn right on Northwoods Boulevard and go 1.4 miles. From here, the boulevard forms a loop; stay to

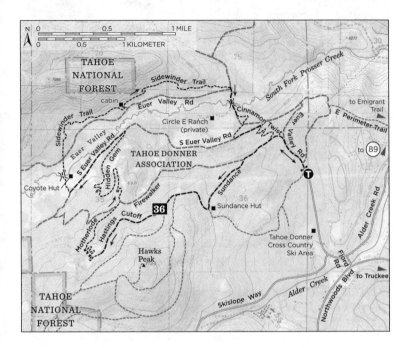

the right and go 2.5 miles to Fjord Road. Turn right on Fjord Road then take a quick left at the T-junction onto Alder Creek Road. In 0.7 mile park at the end of the pavement in the pullout by the locked gate.

MILEAGE LOG

0.0 From the parking area, head north, around the gate, onto Euer Valley Rd.

0.3 Turn left onto a road marked Sundance. You will see the top of Cinnamon Twist on your right in a few hundred feet; this is where you will end the loop. Continue straight and climb, staying on Sundance.

1.0 At the Sundance Hut, turn right onto Hastings Cutoff. Stay on Hastings Cutoff, don't make any turns, as it contours around the north side of Hawks Peak.

2.1 The doubletrack begins to narrow and turns into a wide, recently machine-built singletrack—Motherlode—with a rolling and winding descent.

Dropping into the Euer Valley on the Hidden Gem Trail

3.1 Ride straight across the fire road called Firewalker and begin the descent of Hidden Gem—a narrower singletrack that descends the rest of the way into Euer Valley.

4.4 The singletrack ends on doubletrack of South Euer Valley Rd. Turn left.

5.0 Take a right turn and drop down into the large meadow of Euer Valley.

5.2 Cross over the creek on a bridge constructed over several large corrugated pipes and continue across the meadow.

5.3 The singletrack crosses Euer Valley Rd. on the north side of the meadow. Stay on the singletrack, now called the Sidewinder Trail, that parallels the meadow as it heads east.

6.1 Turn left by an old cabin to stay on the singletrack.

7.0 When the singletrack ends, turn right and head south on Euer Valley Rd., crossing a bridge over the creek.

7.2 Turn left onto the lower part of Cinnamon Twist and begin climbing.

7.4 Cross the dirt road and continue climbing on the singletrack.

7.6 Turn left on the dirt road and follow it east.

7.8 Turn right onto the upper part of the Cinnamon Twist climb.

8.3 Turn left onto the Sundance dirt road and follow it to Euer Valley Rd. and back to the parking area

8.6 Arrive back at the parking area.

OPTIONS

The options for riding in this area are somewhat limitless, though the route described above makes an excellent starting point. Those with energy to spare may want to do multiple laps or make a diversion up to Hawks Peak or the Drifter Hut from Hastings Cutoff. These trails are also easily linked via the East Perimeter Trail to the Emigrant Trail (Route 38) or the Donner Lake Rim Trail (Route 35) for a much longer ride. Those looking to shorten this ride may do so by making a right turn at mile 4.4 on South Euer Valley Road to reach Cinnamon Twist at mile 7.6 as noted above. You can also opt to ride Euer Valley Road and skip the Sidewinder singletrack to save a little time and distance.

37 PROSSER HILL

LOOP

Trail Type: 100% singletrack (wide OHV singletrack)
Distance: 6.9 miles
Elevation Gain/Loss: 1380/1380 feet
High Point: 7152 feet
Ride Time: 1–2 hours
Technical Difficulty: Intermediate

Fitness Intensity: Strenuous
Season: Late spring–fall
Maps: Adventure Maps, Lake Tahoe Basin Trail Map, 2015 version; USGS 7.5-minute, Truckee, Hobart Mills
GPS: 39°23'12.42" N, -120°11'9.18" W

OVERVIEW

Despite the fact that all of the trails on Prosser Hill are OHV (off-highway vehicle) friendly, these wide singletracks are still a great ride on your mountain bike. Easily accessible, this area is a backyard ride for residents of the Prosser Lakeview or Tahoe Donner neighborhoods. Because a variety of other trails link into this small network, there are numerous ways to ride this area, but one of the best is to climb the Animal Trail up to Animal Crackers, then ride up to the top of Prosser Hill, and descend all the way back to the staging area. The descent from the top of Prosser Hill is nearly 3 miles and 1200 vertical feet of fast riding. Despite its relatively short length, this loop has a lot of

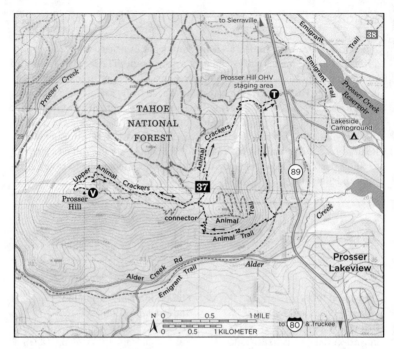

steep climbing and definitely qualifies as strenuous. It is important to note that these trails are frequently ridden by motocross bikes and you may encounter them on the trail. It is also worth mentioning that the trail conditions may be affected by motocross use and at times may be extra loose and rocky.

GETTING THERE

From the eastern junction of CA 89 and Interstate 80 in Truckee, travel north on CA 89 for 3.5 miles. Turn left into the Prosser Hill OHV staging area parking lot, immediately across CA 89 from the entrance to the Lakeside Campground, and park here.

MILEAGE LOG

0.0 From the staging area, head west on the wide singletrack that is the bottom of the Animal Crackers Trail.

0.1 Turn left (south) on the singletrack that contours around the east side of Prosser Hill.

1.1 Turn right at this five-way intersection with the Emigrant Trail and a dirt road and begin the climb up the Animal Trail.

2.2 After some steep climbing and a lot of tight, uphill switchbacks, the trail begins to level out. Turn left onto the narrow connector singletrack that continues uphill. This short trail connects from the top of the Animal Trail over to the Animal Crackers Trail. If you begin descending on the Animal Trail, you have gone too far.

2.4 After crossing over the ridge, arrive at a junction with the Animal Crackers Trail; take a left.

2.5 Bear right on a narrow singletrack and connect to Upper Animal Crackers for

Cruising down the Animal Crackers Trail on Prosser Hill

the duration of the climb to the top of Prosser Hill. You can go straight here, but it is a very steep, loose, and rocky climb to the top.

3.9 Arrive at the top of the climb and enjoy great views in all directions. Turn around and descend the way you came.

5.2 Bear right off of the Upper Animal Crackers section and over to the lower section you came up on.

5.4 At the junction with the connector from the Animal Trail, bear left, downhill, and continue on the wide singletrack of Animal Crackers all the way back down to the OHV staging area.

6.9 Arrive at the parking area.

OPTIONS

You can ride up Animal Crackers and do this ride as an out-and-back with a somewhat more gradual climb. You can also opt to drop down the Animal Trail on your return from Prosser Hill for a steeper and more technical descent to the parking area by turning right at mile 5.4. To get some extra mileage, it is easy to link up with the Emigrant Trail (Route 38) at mile 1.1, and you can also follow that trail west to the East Perimeter Trail to link into the Tahoe Donner trail system in Euer Valley (Route 36).

38 EMIGRANT TRAIL

OUT-AND-BACK

Trail Type: 100% singletrack
Distance: 18.2 miles
Elevation Gain/Loss: 1700/1700 feet
High Point: 6089 feet
Ride Time: 1.5–3 hours
Technical Difficulty: Beginner

Fitness Intensity: Moderate
Season: Early spring–late fall
Maps: Adventure Maps, Lake Tahoe Basin Trail Map, 2015 version; USGS 7.5-minute, Hobart Mills
GPS: 39°23′53.83″ N, -120°11′12.21″ W

OVERVIEW

The Emigrant Trail, officially known as the Commemorative Emigrant Trail, roughly follows the path historically used by emigrants traveling through the Sierra Nevada in the mid-1800s. This rolling singletrack trail winds through beautiful high desert terrain for 9 miles between Prosser Creek and Stampede Reservoir. Numerous short climbs bring you from grassy meadows over the crests of small hills covered in mixed conifer forest. The generally smooth trail is beginner friendly, with occasional moderately challenging rock gardens that help add a little excitement. However, those seeking thrills or technical challenge will be better off riding many of the other routes listed in this guide.

From the trailhead, the route is quite easy to follow. The trail crosses several dirt and paved roads over its course, but in all cases is obvious and clearly visible on the other side. As an out-and-back ride, the Emigrant Trail dips

Riding above Prosser Creek on the Commemorative Emigrant Trail (Oscar Havens)

and dives through grassy fields, sagebrush meadows, and open forests for as far as you want; take it all the way to Stampede Reservoir or turn around whenever you like. Situated just east of the Sierra Crest and lower in elevation relative to other rides in the area, the Emigrant Trail is one of the first to melt out in spring and one of the last to get snow covered in the fall, making this one of the first and last rides of the season for area residents.

GETTING THERE

From the eastern junction of Interstate 80 and CA 89 in Truckee, travel north on CA 89 for 4.5 miles. Turn right onto Hobart Mills Road, then take the first right into the new Emigrant Trail parking area.

MILEAGE LOG

0.0 From the parking area, head southeast on the Emigrant Trail singletrack.

0.6 Bear right on the dirt road for about 100 feet before getting back onto singletrack on the left; it's an obvious turn.

0.9 Cross the pavement of Old Hwy. 89.

1.8 Cross Old Reno Rd. at the top of the climb.

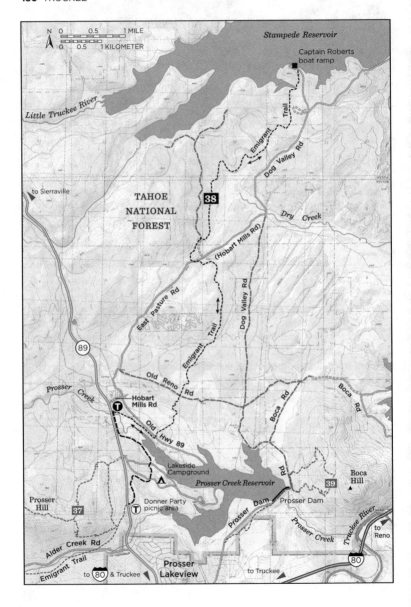

3.8 Reach the highest point in the ride, 6089 feet.

4.6 Cross East Pasture Rd. (Hobart Mills Rd.). Be sure to look both ways as this paved road does see vehicle traffic.

5.0 Cross a dirt road.

8.3 The trail forks; take a left toward Captain Roberts boat ramp on Stampede Reservoir. (The right-hand trail goes to a small dirt parking area off Dog Valley Rd.)

8.6 Reach an arm of Stampede Reservoir. At high water you'll need to ride around this to continue on the trail; at low water you can ride straight across.

9.1 Arrive at the boat ramp. Turn around here and ride back the way you came.

13.6 Cross East Pasture Rd. (Hobart Mills Rd.).

16.4 Cross Old Reno Rd.

17.3 Cross Old Hwy. 89.

18.2 Arrive back at the parking area.

OPTIONS

To add 2.7 miles of riding onto each end of this route, you can begin your ride at the Donner Party picnic area. This trailhead is 1.5 miles south of the trailhead listed above (and 2.9 miles north of I-80) on the east side of CA 89. This section of trail winds along the east side of CA 89 to Prosser Creek. Cross the creek on the CA 89 bridge and pick up the route described above. You can also add some mileage by following the Emigrant Trail farther west to link into Prosser Hill (Route 37) or along Alder Creek toward Tahoe Donner and Euer Valley (Route 36). A few miles of dirt road riding to the east on the Old Reno Road, Dog Valley Road, and Prosser Dam Road will also lead you over to Lloyds Loop (Route 39).

39 LLOYDS LOOP

LOOP

Trail Type: 90% singletrack, 5% pavement, 5% doubletrack

Distance: 5.8 miles
Elevation Gain/Loss: 600/600 feet

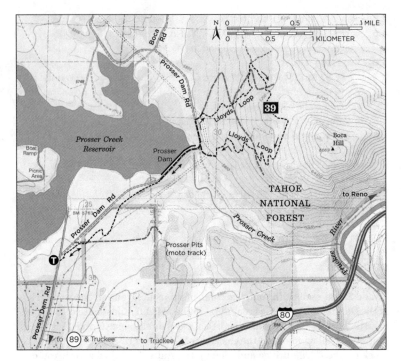

High Point: 6301 feet

Ride Time: 45 minutes–1.5 hours

Technical Difficulty: Intermediate

Fitness Intensity: Easy

Season: Early spring–late fall

Maps: USGS 7.5-minute, Truckee, Hobart Mills, Martis Peak, Boca

GPS: 39°22'9.31" N, -120°9'17.97" W

OVERVIEW

The Lloyds Loop sits on the western flank of Boca Hill, sandwiched between the Prosser Creek and Boca reservoirs. Just three miles from downtown Truckee and close to several Truckee subdivisions, this loop is just out the back door for many local residents. For others, it is a once- or twice-a-year affair during the spring or late fall when other higher elevation trails remain snowbound. A ride of Lloyds is almost like a spring rite of passage for me and is among my first rides of the year. This loop is nice because you get a flat warm-up before you cross the dam, followed by a great, albeit short, singletrack loop. Unlike other low-elevation rides in the area, Lloyds actually has some sustained climbing; it's still not much, but it's all at once.

You can ride the loop either way, but clockwise is more popular for easier climbing and a more exciting descent. You may see dirt bikers in this parking area as it is also used to access the Prosser Pits, a motocross area below the Prosser Dam.

Enjoying springtime on Boca Hill

GETTING THERE

From the eastern junction of CA 89 and Interstate 80 in Truckee, travel north on CA 89 for 0.3 mile to the second roundabout and turn right onto Prosser Dam Road. Follow Prosser Dam Road for 1.6 miles to the end of the pavement and park in the dirt parking area on the left.

MILEAGE LOG

0.0 From the parking area, ride across the road and start heading northeast down Prosser Dam Rd. The singletrack starts almost immediately on the right and parallels the road.

0.2 Take a right on this dirt road, then take a left in a couple hundred feet back onto the singletrack. Stay left at all the intersections after this to stay on the trail that parallels Prosser Dam Rd.

1.0 The trail joins Prosser Dam Rd.; follow it across the dam.

1.4 To begin the loop clockwise, stay on the main road as it curves to the left.

1.6 Take a right onto a dirt road.

1.7 Turn right onto the singletrack at this unsigned junction.

2.0 Cross a dirt road.

2.4 Cross another dirt road.

2.7 Take a right at this intersection.

3.0 Arrive at the top of the climb and the beginning of the descent.

3.8 Cross a dirt road.

4.2 Turn right at the end of the singletrack and head back toward Prosser Dam Rd.

4.4 Turn left on Prosser Dam Rd. and ride back across the dam (or continue straight to do another lap or two).

4.8 After crossing the dam, turn left onto the singletrack and ride it back the way you came.

5.8 Arrive at the parking area.

OPTIONS

Because this is a relatively short ride, people will often ride the loop several times or in both directions. It is also common for local riders to combine this route with nearby trails like Prosser Hill (Route 37) or the Emigrant Trail (Route 38) to make a longer ride, or to ride to it from town. The network of dirt roads around the reservoirs offers many miles of pedaling for anyone looking to spend more time in the saddle.

40 SAWTOOTH RIDGE

LOLLIPOP LOOP

Trail Type: 100% singletrack
Distance: 10.5 miles
Elevation Gain/Loss: 700/700 feet
High Point: 6425 feet
Ride Time: 1–2.5 hours
Technical Difficulty: Intermediate

Fitness Intensity: Moderate
Season: Late spring–fall
Maps: Adventure Maps, Lake Tahoe Basin Trail Map, 2015 version; USGS 7.5-minute, Truckee
GPS: 39°18'36.06" N, -120°11'29.63" W

OVERVIEW

Situated just south of Truckee on a plateau above the Truckee River canyon, the Sawtooth Ridge Trail is an easy, rolling singletrack lollipop loop. This

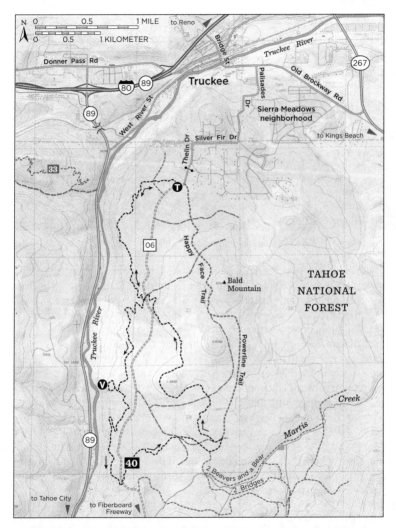

10.5-mile route has minimal climbing, only 700 feet or so, but the occasionally rough and rocky trail can sometimes make it feel like more. The loop itself can be ridden in either direction, and a number of other trails in the

Above the Truckee River Canyon on the Sawtooth Ridge Trail (Oscar Havens)

area can be explored to add time and distance to this ride. Sawtooth's low elevation, relative to other rides in the area, lends itself to being among the first trails in the area to be free of snow in the spring and the last to be covered in the fall. This area also is easily accessed by Truckee residents, making it popular for before- and after-work rides and trail runs.

To begin the route, jump on the singletrack by the sign and map at the trailhead and ride south on the lollipop stick for about 2 miles to the start of the loop. You can ride the loop in either direction, and if you have time I'd suggest trying both ways to decide which you like best (it is described here in the counterclockwise direction). Several viewpoints along the way offer views of the Truckee River and the Pacific Crest, providing great spots to stop and take a break along the way. The trail crosses several dirt roads over the 6.8-mile loop's course and in all cases continues on the other side. There are also trail maps and signs at both the south and north ends of the loop where the trail crosses the 06 Fire Road. Once back at the start of the loop, head north on the lollipop stick back to the trailhead.

GETTING THERE

From the junction of Donner Pass Road and Bridge Street in Truckee, head south on Bridge Street and follow it as it curves left and turns into Old

Brockway Road. In 0.3 mile turn right on Palisades Drive and head south. Follow Palisades Drive for 0.9 mile and turn right on Silver Fir Drive, following it for 0.4 mile before turning left onto Thelin Drive. In 0.2 mile, take the first right onto the 06 Fire Road and follow it for 0.3 mile to the Sawtooth Ridge trailhead parking area on the right. If the 06 Fire Road gate is locked, you can park near it and pedal the short distance to the trailhead.

MILEAGE LOG

0.0 Jump on the singletrack that starts next to the trail map and sign. The trail initially heads west before turning south.

0.3 Cross a dirt road.

1.0 The trail runs along the top of a bluff above the Truckee River.

1.9 Reach the end of the lollipop stick. Turn right to ride the loop counterclockwise.

3.3 A short spur trail leads out to a cool viewpoint above the river.

4.7 The trail crosses the 06 Fire Rd. at the south end of the loop.

5.5 Cross a dirt road.

5.7 Cross another dirt road.

5.9 At the junction with the 2 Bridges Trail on the right, stay straight.

6.0 At the junction with a fire road, turn left onto the dirt road. (Going straight here leads to the Powerline Trail.)

6.1 Turn right to get back onto the singletrack and begin a steady but very mellow climb to the trail's high point.

6.7 Cross a dirt road.

7.4 Reach the trail's high point at 6425 feet.

8.6 Ride straight across the 06 Fire Rd. back to the start of the loop. Turn right to head north on the lollipop stick back to the trailhead.

10.5 Arrive at the trailhead.

OPTIONS

There are a number of other trails in this area, and they can easily be linked up with the Sawtooth Ridge Trail to make your ride any length you want. At mile 5.9 you can do a loop on the 2 Bridges and 2 Beavers and a Bear trails or continue on the Schaeffer Creek Trail for an out-and-back, both great options that offer narrow, creekside singletrack. At mile 6.0 you have the option of jumping onto the Powerline Trail and then descending the Happy Face Trail to return to the trailhead.

DOWNIEVILLE AND GRAEAGLE

The quaint mining town of Downieville, California, is located in the heart of the Sierra Nevada foothills on CA 49 at the confluence of the Downie River and the North Fork of the Yuba River at an elevation of 2966 feet. While the gold mining boom may have come and gone, this sleepy little town is now home to some of the finest riding in the state with trails that drop 4000 vertical feet over the course of 15 miles from Packer Saddle down to Main Street in Downieville. Known for the world-famous Downieville Downhill and the Downieville Classic mountain bike race, this area features an amazing network of trails that will have you grinning from ear to ear and coming back time and time again.

The retirement and golf community of Graeagle, California, lies just east of the Pacific Crest on the north end of the Gold Lake Highway. While the town may be well known for its golf courses, it is also becoming a destination for mountain bikers, especially when coupled with the nearby riding in Downieville. The Mills Peak Trail (Route 42) is the main riding attraction above Graeagle, but a plethora of other adventurous, and I mean adventurous, riding exists in and around the Lakes basin.

Opposite: *Diving into a turn on the Sunrise Flow Trail near Packer Saddle below the Sierra Buttes*

41 DOWNIEVILLE

SHUTTLE

Trail Type: 86% singletrack,
7% doubletrack, 7% pavement
Distance: 15 miles
Elevation Gain/Loss: 1180/5350 feet
High Point: 7065 feet
Ride Time: 1–3 hours
Technical Difficulty: Expert
Fitness Intensity: Moderate

Season: Summer–fall
Maps: Sierra Buttes Trail Stewardship,
Downieville and Lakes Basin Trail
Map; USGS 7.5-minute, Downieville,
Sierra City, Gold Lake
GPS: 39°36'52.39" N, -120°39'59.57" W;
Downieville: 39°33'36.78" N,
-120°49'44.71" W

OVERVIEW

Around Downieville, the same trails that miners cut into the steep river canyons to access their claims have become a recreational gold mine of sorts, bringing mountain bikers from around the world to ride this world-class network of trails. The most popular descent is the renowned Downieville Downhill, a 15-mile, 4000-vertical-foot descent, made famous by the Downieville Classic Mountain Bike Race, known for being one of the toughest point-to-point bike races in the country.

Downieville area trails are maintained by the Sierra Buttes Trail Stewardship, and they have done an amazing job of keeping them in great riding shape year after year. The group is also responsible for recent trail construction, including the Upper Butcher Ranch singletrack and the Packer Saddle Loop Trail, which includes the Sunrise Flow Trail.

Yuba Expeditions (www.yubaexpeditions.com) and Downieville Outfitters (www.downievilleoutfitters.com) are the two Downieville-based bike shops and shuttle operations running regularly scheduled shuttles from town to the top of Packer Saddle. For the route and the options described here, I recommend using one of these shuttle services to reach the trailhead if you are not self-shuttling.

All Downieville rides start from Packer Saddle on either the classic Sunrise Trail or the new Sunrise Flow Trail. You'll follow Sunrise Flow, which is a nice, wide singletrack with whoops and well-made berms that flows its way down to reconnect with the Sunrise Trail, and then continue down to Butcher Ranch

Picking a line through the "waterfall" on the Butcher Ranch Trail

Road. Once you arrive at Butcher Ranch Road, you have options. For this route, take the new Upper Butcher singletrack down to the top of the Butcher Ranch Trail descent. This narrow, winding singletrack stretching for 2.4 miles between Butcher Ranch Road and the top of Butcher Ranch Trail is the most popular way down and arguably the most fun.

The next segment on the Butcher Ranch Trail, part of the classic Downieville Downhill, is fast, rocky, and so much fun. From the ravine at the top of the Butcher Ranch Trail to the Pauley Creek Bridge is 3.5 miles of beautiful, challenging riding. After the bridge there is a short climb that leads to the top of the 2nd and 3rd Divide trails. This route passes the top of 2nd Divide and drops into the eye-watering, fast descent of 3rd Divide for 2 miles down to Lavezzola Road. The gravity-fed speed of this trail makes the 2 miles go by in a hurry. Once you hit Lavezzola Road, turn left and descend for a mile to the top of the 1st Divide. The last stretch of this descent on 1st Divide is

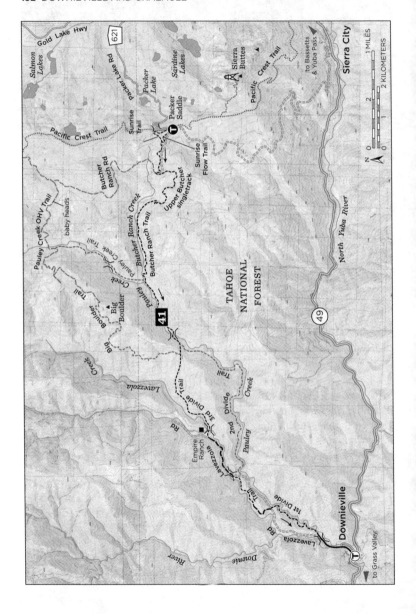

mostly singletrack, but it does involve a short stretch of doubletrack riding. While the 1st Divide is flatter in comparison with the other trails, there is significant exposure above the creek at many points. After 3 miles, the trail ends on the paved Lavezzola Road, which you'll follow for the last mile into Downieville.

GETTING THERE

If you are self-shuttling, leave your shuttle car in Downieville in either of the public parking lots that are right in the center of town near the Downieville grocery store and the confluence of the Downie and North Yuba rivers.

To reach the start of the ride from Downieville, head east on CA 49 for 17.5 miles to Bassetts. Turn left on Gold Lake Highway (County Route S620) and follow it for 1.3 miles. Turn left on Packer Lake Road (CR 621) and in 0.3 mile take the first right to stay on Packer Lake Road. Continue uphill for 2.6 miles, and take the left fork on CR 621 at Packer Lake. Continue uphill for another 1.3 miles and after a couple of really steep switchbacks bear left and stay on the paved road, CR 621. Just after cresting the top of the hill, at the junction with Butcher Ranch Road, park in the large dirt parking area on the left at Packer Saddle.

MILEAGE LOG

0.0 Begin on the Sunrise Trail just north of the parking area and across the road at the top of Packer Saddle, by the shuttle drop-off.

0.1 The classic Sunrise Trail continues to the right and the new Sunrise Flow Trail goes left. The trails combine in 0.6 (Flow) and 1.0 (Sunrise) miles, respectively, and then it is another 0.8 mile down to Butcher Ranch Rd. For this route, go left onto Sunrise Flow.

1.5 Ride straight across Butcher Ranch Rd. onto the new Upper Butcher singletrack.

3.9 After 2.4 miles of steady pedaling on this singletrack, cross the ravine that marks the top of the Butcher Ranch Trail descent. The trail now parallels Butcher Ranch Creek on some classic, rocky, and challenging singletrack.

5.1 Reach the infamous waterfall corner. There are number of hard but rideable lines through this zone; use extra caution when the rocks are wet!

5.7 At the junction with the bottom of the Pauley Creek Trail, turn left and continue the Butcher Ranch descent. There are short sections of exposure above the creek, so use caution.

7.3   Cross the distinctive bridge over Pauley Creek. This is a good spot for a mid-ride break. A short climb begins here that leads to the top of the 2nd and 3rd Divide trails.

7.7   Arrive at the junction of the 2nd and 3rd Divide trails. Continue straight for 3rd Divide.

7.8   At the top of the 3rd Divide descent, make sure your brakes are working for the 2.0 miles of almost pure descent. One short, punchy climb near the bottom, known as the Wall, is the only place you'll need to pedal until you reach the bridge.

9.8   Cross Lavezzola Creek on the bridge and pedal a very short distance to Lavezzola Rd. Turn left on Lavezzola Rd. and pedal through Empire Ranch.

9.9   Begin the fast descent down Lavezzola Rd.; watch for vehicles.

11.0   After crossing back over Lavezzola Creek, bear right onto 1st Divide. This section of 1st Divide is relatively exposed above the creek, so use caution. The trail turns to doubletrack for a short stretch before crossing Lavezzola Rd. again.

12.6   Cross Lavezzola Rd. yet again.

12.8   Look for the singletrack to pick up on the right; it will sneak up on you.

14.0   The trail ends at Lavezzola Rd.; bear left. Cross the bridge and continue on Main St. into town. Be sure to stop at stop signs.

15.0   Reach the end of the ride at the confluence of the rivers, public parking, and the Yuba Expeditions and Downieville Outfitters shops.

OPTIONS

There are a number of ways to descend from Packer Saddle all the way down to Downieville. The classic Sunrise Trail used to be the only way to start a Downieville lap. This trail is technical and fun and slightly longer—1.9 miles—than Sunrise Flow from the top to Butcher Ranch Road.

At mile 1.5, you can take a right turn, and 3.6 miles of pedaling on Butcher Ranch Road will bring you to the top of Pauley Creek Trail, part of the Downieville Classic Cross-Country course. This trail starts out as a rough OHV (off-highway vehicle) road, passing through a section known as the "baby heads," before crossing Pauley Creek and turning into a fast downhill that parallels the creek down to its junction with the Butcher Ranch Trail in 4.3 miles, for a total of 7.9 miles.

From the bottom of Sunrise, you can also opt to climb up to Big Boulder for an amazing sidehill descent. At the junction with Butcher Ranch Road, turn right on Butcher Ranch Road and continue on the Pauley Creek OHV Trail to the junction with the Pauley Creek and Big Boulder trails at 6.4 miles. Turn right onto the Big Boulder Trail and climb an old OHV road for 2.6 miles and 850 vertical feet. Once you arrive at the top of the climb, a short descent on a rough, rocky road leads to one of the sweetest sidehill singletracks imaginable and a 3.7-mile descent to the top of 3rd Divide. From the bottom of the Sunrise Trail to the top of 3rd Divide via Big Boulder is 12.7 miles.

At mile 7.7, you can opt to ride 2nd Divide instead of 3rd Divide. A more technical route, 2nd Divide contours the opposite side of the ridge from 3rd Divide and is composed mostly of an old mining trail, which at times has significant exposure above the creek below. While it involves more pedaling than 3rd Divide, the 2nd Divide generally trends downhill and offers a technical challenge to even the most talented riders over its 4.5-mile length, which ends at Lavezzola Road just above the junction with 1st Divide. Drop down to 1st Divide and rejoin the route described above at mile 11.0.

The lower trails—1st, 2nd, and 3rd Divide—also offer shorter options for loops from Downieville in spring and fall when the upper portions of this ride are still snowbound.

42 MILLS PEAK

OUT-AND-BACK

Trail Type: 80% singletrack, 20% doubletrack
Distance: 17.6 miles
Elevation Gain/Loss: 2900/2900 feet
High Point: 7311 feet
Ride Time: 2.5–4.5 hours
Technical Difficulty: Advanced

Fitness Intensity: Strenuous
Season: Summer–fall
Maps: Sierra Buttes Trail Stewardship, Downieville and Lakes Basin Trail Map; USGS 7.5-minute, Gold Lake, Clio, Blairsden
GPS: 39°45'13.59" N, -120°35'55.37" W

OVERVIEW

One of the newest works of trail art created by the prolific trail building and advocacy group known as the Sierra Buttes Trail Stewardship, the Mills Peak Trail climbs and descends nearly 3000 vertical feet between CA 89 and the

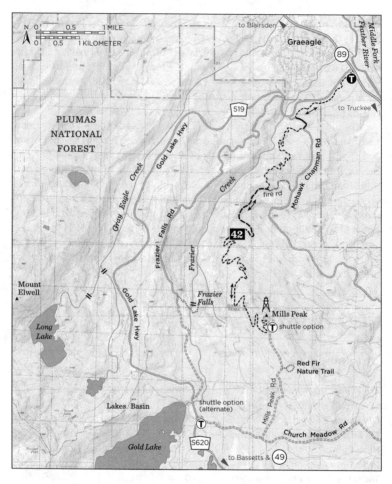

fire lookout at the summit of Mills Peak. Upon its completion, it instantly became the premier ride in this area east of the Pacific Crest thanks to its well-built singletrack, which is as nice to climb as it is to descend.

The trail is primarily singletrack that winds its way along the north/northeast ridge of Mills Peak through a relatively dense conifer forest. It is littered

The Sierra Buttes serve as a picturesque backdrop on this rocky corner of the Mills Peak Trail.

with moderately technical rock gardens that present fun challenges, but these are rideable both up and down. The upper and lower portions of the trail are broken up by a 1.5-mile stretch of doubletrack fire road that is a grind on the way up and can be scary fast on the way down, so be on the lookout for other riders. A singletrack reroute is being planned for this section, and once in place, it will make the trail almost 100 percent singletrack and even better than it already is.

The fire lookout sits atop a rocky outcrop on the 7311-foot summit of Mills Peak and commands an impressive 360-degree view of the Sierra Valley to the east, the Lakes basin and Sierra Buttes to the south and west, and Mount Lassen far to the north. This fire lookout is one of several in the area that is still in use and is often occupied by a US Forest Service fire spotter.

GETTING THERE

From Graeagle, drive south on CA 89 for 1.4 miles; from Truckee, drive north on CA 89 for 44 miles. The Mills Peak trailhead is on the west side of CA 89 in a dirt pullout, just 100 yards south of the junction with the Gold Lake Highway.

MILEAGE LOG

0.0 From the parking area, head west on the singletrack.
1.3 Turn left on Mohawk Chapman Rd. and climb for 0.3 mile on pavement.
1.6 Turn right off the pavement onto the singletrack next to the Mills Peak Trail sign.
3.6 Turn right on the fire road and climb for 1.5 miles.
5.2 Continue straight as the fire road turns back into singletrack.
8.8 Arrive at the top of the climb and the Mills Peak fire lookout. To return to the parking area, descend the approach route.
12.4 Arrive at the top of the fire road. Be careful and watch for others on this descent.
13.9 Turn left off the fire road back onto the singletrack. This intersection is marked with a sign but will sneak up on you on the descent regardless.
15.9 Turn left on Mohawk Chapman Rd. and descend for 0.3 mile.
16.2 Turn right onto the singletrack at the bottom of the hill.
17.6 Return to the parking area at CA 89.

OPTIONS

Shuttling puts this route in the Easy category, making it a 35-minute to 1.5-hour ride and 2897 feet of almost pure descent. Leave a vehicle at the CA 89 parking area described above and drive 8.8 miles southwest up Gold Lake Highway and turn left on Church Meadow Road. Follow it for 1 mile, turn left on Mills Peak Road, and continue for 2 miles to the end of the road and the Mills Peak fire lookout. Many people opt to park at the beginning of the dirt roads and pedal up them to avoid the dirt portion of the shuttle drive.

For the ride from the fire lookout, drop in by the picnic table next to the trail sign. At mile 3.6, reach the fire road and follow it for 1.5 miles to the left turn back onto the singletrack. At mile 7.1, take the left turn onto Mohawk Chapman Road and at mile 7.4 turn right onto the singletrack to reach the parking area and your shuttle vehicle at 8.8 miles.

No regular shuttle services operate on this side of the crest, but special arrangements can be made with shuttle operations in nearby Downieville.

This ride can also be turned into a 19.5-mile loop, including a 10.7-mile climb, by incorporating secondary or dirt roads that see very little traffic. From the parking area on CA 89, climb west up Gold Lake Highway for 1.7 miles, turn left on Frazier Creek Road, and climb it for 5.7 miles until it intersects Gold Lake Highway again. Turn left onto Gold Lake Highway and follow it for 0.3 mile to the junction with Church Meadow Road. Turn left, follow it for 1 mile, then turn left on Mills Peak Road and ride for 2 more miles to the end of the road and the fire lookout. From there, follow the route described above.

SIERRA NEVADA FOOTHILLS

The western foothills of the Sierra Nevada offer a variety of excellent mountain bike rides. Generally speaking, residents of the greater Tahoe area frequent these trails in the spring, fall, and winter when the higher elevation riding is prohibitively snowy or cold, while local residents ride them year round. Located 65 miles west of Truckee, historic Auburn, California, has a number of excellent rides, and the Foresthill Divide Loop (Route 45) is among the most popular. Located very close to town, it offers a great, rolling, cross-country ride with a number of options, including the Culvert and Confluence trails, to link up with. Hidden Falls Regional Park is a new public park in Auburn that features a wealth of multiuse trails and is worth a stop as well, but be warned that this park is extremely popular and can be crowded at times.

Just 27 miles north of Auburn is the small town of Nevada City. There are quite a few excellent rides in this area, and the routes described in this guidebook only scratch the surface of the potential here. A vibrant community of local mountain bikers and a growing trail network are making this one of the more popular riding destinations in the Sierra foothills, with the Scotts Flat Trail (Route 43) and the Pioneer Trail (Route 44) among the favorites.

At the southern end of this region, near Pollock Pines, the Sly Park Recreation Area offers the closest foothills riding to the South Lake Tahoe area on trails around Jenkinson Lake and Fleming Meadows (Routes 46 and 47).

Opposite: *The Scotts Flat Trail is one of many great places to ride in the foothills west of Lake Tahoe.* (Heather Benson)

43 SCOTTS FLAT TRAIL

LOOP

Trail Type: 60% singletrack, 40% pavement
Distance: 9.2 miles
Elevation Gain/Loss: 980/980 feet
High Point: 3464 feet
Ride Time: 1–2 hours

Technical Difficulty: Beginner
Fitness Intensity: Easy
Season: Year-round
Map: USGS 7.5-minute, North Bloomfield
GPS: 39°17′12.80″ N, -120°56′41.14″ W

OVERVIEW

The Scotts Flat Trail, created by the Bicyclists of Nevada County (BONC), local volunteers, and community groups, was made with mountain bikers in mind and it shows in the entertaining route and well-constructed berms and corners. Now a flowing singletrack that drops from CA 20 to the Scotts Flat Reservoir, it replaced the old, eroded, and decommissioned Scotts Drop Trail and has quickly become one of the more popular sections of trail in the area.

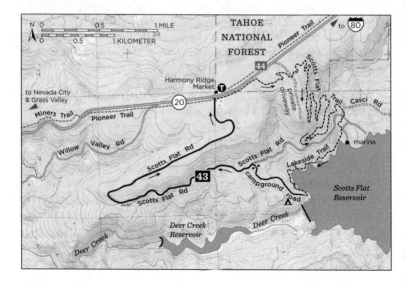

The ride starts just across CA 20 from the Harmony Ridge Market and follows a circuitous route down the hillside with plenty of whoops, berms, and corners. Once you get down to the Scotts Flat Reservoir, the route follows the Lakeside Trail to the campground for the return on paved roads to the starting point.

GETTING THERE

From Nevada City, travel approximately 5 miles east on CA 20 to the Harmony Ridge Market. A trail user parking area and Pioneer Trail trailhead are on the east side of the market.

Hitting a log ride near the top of the Scotts Flat Trail (Heather Benson)

MILEAGE LOG

0.0 From the parking area, cross CA 20 and turn left (east) on the trail that parallels the road.

0.3 Turn right at the sign for the Scotts Flat Trail.

1.0 Cross a paved private driveway; the descent begins.

3.9 Cross Casci Rd. and then Scotts Flat Rd.

4.2 Turn hard right on the Lakeside Trail; a left turn brings you to the marina. Ride along the edge of the reservoir to the dam.

5.4 By the dam, turn right into the Scotts Flat Lake Campground. Ride uphill through the campground on the paved access road.

6.0 Go through the entrance to the campground, turn left on Scotts Flat Rd., and follow it for 3 miles.

9.1 Scotts Flat Rd. intersects CA 20.

9.2 Return to the parking area.

OPTIONS

While many people ride the Scotts Flat Trail as part of a loop or a longer route, it was designed to be ridden in both directions, so don't be surprised to see uphill traffic. An out-and-back is a good option if you are looking to stay on dirt for the whole ride. If you're interested in a longer route, Scotts Flat is close enough to Nevada City to pedal up to it via the Snow Mountain Ditch–Willow Valley Road climb with a return to town along the Miners Trail. Scotts Flat is also ideally situated to be combined with the Pioneer Trail (Route 44).

44 PIONEER TRAIL

OUT-AND-BACK

Trail Type: 70% singletrack, 30% doubletrack
Distance: 16.8 miles
Elevation Gain/Loss: 1300/1300 feet
High Point: 4253 feet
Ride Time: 2–3 hours
Technical Difficulty: Beginner

Fitness Intensity: Moderate
Season: Early spring–late fall (sometimes year-round)
Maps: USGS 7.5-minute, North Bloomfield, Washington
GPS: 39°17'12.80" N, -120°56'41.14" W

OVERVIEW

This classic foothills ride parallels CA 20 just east of Nevada City and is an excellent introduction to the trails in this area. The relatively mellow route follows the spine of a long, flat ridge it shares with CA 20 and therefore has very gradual elevation change over its course. It is generally smooth and non-technical, although a number of root-filled sections and the occasional rock garden will keep your eyes on the trail. CA 20 remains within earshot for the ride's entirety, and at times you will be riding singletrack within feet of the edge of the road.

The Pioneer Trail is generally ridden as an out-and-back from the Harmony Ridge Market, but it can also be shuttled by anyone looking to do a point-to-point ride (see Options). The route described here features roughly

Jumping into a series of swooping turns on the Pioneer Trail

8 miles of the Pioneer Trail each way, but the entire trail is approximately 25 miles long from the market to its eastern terminus near Bowman Lake. This is a popular multi-use trail, so don't be surprised to see runners, walkers, and equestrians out enjoying it.

GETTING THERE

From Nevada City, travel approximately 5 miles east on CA 20 to the Harmony Ridge Market. A trail user parking area and Pioneer Trail trailhead are on the east side of the market.

MILEAGE LOG

0.0 Head east out of the trailhead parking area, climbing gradually on the Pioneer Trail. The beginning of this ride varies from wide singletrack to doubletrack, eventually narrowing down to singletrack.

2.5 Continue straight across Conservation Rd. Stay on the Pioneer Trail, which has now become a narrower singletrack along the edge of CA 20. The trail will cross a number of side roads and driveways, but remains quite easy to follow.

6.5 Just before the White Cloud Campground, cross CA 20 and continue on the Pioneer Trail. After a short descent the trail becomes relatively level as it follows an old flume for a while before becoming a bit more interesting as it dips and dives through the dense pine forest.

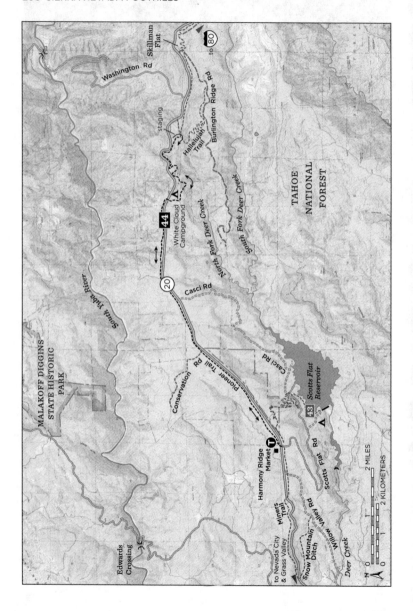

8.4   In a large clearing known as "staging," the singletrack empties out into the clearing and continues on the far side. This is the turnaround point for this route. The Hallelujah Trail, which comes off the Burlington Ridge Rd. from Skillman Flat, also ends in this clearing.

10.3   Cross CA 20 just past the White Cloud Campground and pick up the trail again on the north side of the road.

14.3   Cross Conservation Rd. There are a number of optional small jumps and swooping turns just past this intersection that are fun when you are heading west.

16.8   Arrive at the parking area.

OPTIONS

For a longer route, you can ride up from Nevada City on the Snow Mountain Ditch to Willow Valley Road to start a ride on the Pioneer Trail and return with a descent on the Miners Trail. Another great option is to do a point-to-point ride on the Pioneer Trail from the Omega rest stop to the bottom of the Scotts Flat Trail (Route 43), leaving a shuttle car at the Harmony Ridge Market.

45 FORESTHILL DIVIDE

LOLLIPOP LOOP

Trail Type: 100% singletrack
Distance: 16.8 miles
Elevation Gain/Loss: 2520/2520 feet
High Point: 1933 feet
Ride Time: 1.5–3 hours
Technical Difficulty: Intermediate

Fitness Intensity: Moderate
Season: Year-round
Maps: USGS 7.5-minute, Auburn, Greenwood
GPS: 38°55'58.63" N, 121°0'42.94" W

OVERVIEW

The Foresthill Divide Loop Trail straddles the Foresthill Divide, the ridge that separates the Middle and North Forks of the American River. It is bisected by Foresthill Road and crosses it twice along the way. Following generally smooth, hard-pack singletrack, this rolling cross-country ride

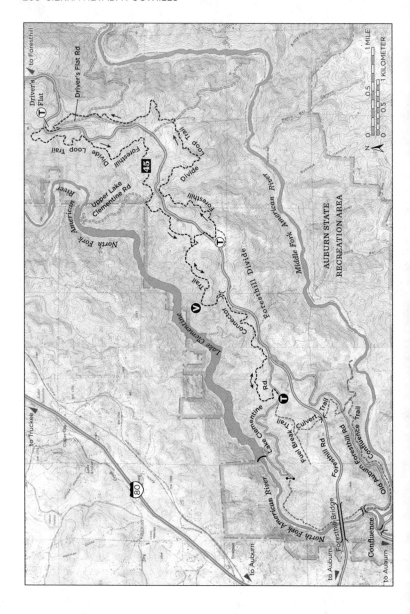

contours the rugged river canyon hillsides through meadows, manzanita bushes, and oak and madrone forests. The 9.6-mile loop has little sustained climbing, but a lot of short, steep climbs and descents that add up to 2500 vertical feet when combined with the 3.6-mile Connector Trail as a lollipop loop. It's equally enjoyable in either direction, so those with the time and energy may want to ride it both ways to find out which they prefer.

There is a vibrant local mountain biking community in the Auburn area, and this is some of the closest good singletrack riding to the Sacramento metropolitan area. With its low elevation, this route is rideable year round, and so it is also quite popular with Tahoe area residents in the winter and spring when the higher elevation trails are unrideable.

Oak trees dominate the landscape along Auburn's Foresthill Divide Loop.

Note that the trails do get slick and muddy after heavy rains in the winter months, and the midsummer heat can also get pretty intense, so plan accordingly.

A few warnings: The dense vegetation and winding trails make for a number of blind corners along this route, so please ride at a sight-distance-appropriate speed and be on the lookout for other riders. Also, trails at this elevation are home to ticks and poison oak. Anyone who is highly allergic to poison oak may want to avoid these trails entirely but especially during the late spring and early summer months.

GETTING THERE

From Interstate 80 in Auburn, take the Auburn Ravine Road and Foresthill exit and head east on Foresthill Road for 3.2 miles. Turn left onto Lake Clementine Road, follow it for 0.6 mile, and park in the dirt pullout on the left. The Fuel Break Trail begins here, and the beginning of the Connector Trail is on the opposite side of the road.

MILEAGE LOG

0.0 Begin on the Connector Trail, a 3.6-mile section that links Lake Clementine Rd. to the Foresthill Divide Loop.

2.2 Cross a bridge at the bottom of a short descent; be careful as it becomes slippery when wet. This is the beginning of a short, steep climb.

2.7 Arrive at a nice viewpoint with a bench overlooking Lake Clementine.

3.6 At the junction with the Foresthill Divide Loop, choose which way you want to ride the loop. I prefer to ride counterclockwise; turn right to do so.

3.8 Ride straight across Foresthill Rd.; use caution as people drive fast on this road.

4.1 After a short climb through a meadow, turn left to stay on the loop. The other trail at this junction is a spur that leads to a parking area on Foresthill Rd.

8.3 The trail crosses Driver's Flat Rd. Pick it up again just uphill on the right side of the parking area.

9.0 The trail pops out onto Foresthill Rd. Turn right and cross when the road is clear. The trail picks back up on the left at the large pullout and parking area known as Driver's Flat. This is roughly the midpoint of the ride and a great spot to take a break.

12.1 Cross Upper Lake Clementine Rd.

13.1 Return to the junction with the Connector Trail. Turn right and enjoy this great section back to the parking area.

13.9 Pass the viewpoint and descend to the bridge.

14.6 Cross the bridge.

16.8 Return to Lake Clementine Rd. and the parking area.

OPTIONS

You can ride the Foresthill Divide Loop alone by parking at one of the alternate trailheads on Foresthill Road. You can also make an additional loop by riding up the Fuel Break Trail from the parking area and descending on the Culvert and Confluence trails to the confluence of the rivers, then following the trail on the east side of the North Fork of the American upstream to Lake Clementine Road, which will take you back to the parking area. It's also an option to add mileage to this route by doing the Foresthill loop twice, once in each direction.

46 SLY PARK AND JENKINSON LAKE

LOOP

Trail Type: 80% singletrack, 20% pavement
Distance: 8.8 miles
Elevation Gain/Loss: 400/400 feet
High Point: 3550 feet
Ride Time: 1–2 hours

Technical Difficulty: Beginner
Fitness Intensity: Easy
Season: Year-round
Map: USGS 7.5-minute, Sly Park
GPS: 38°43'29.49" N, -120°34'10.50" W

OVERVIEW

Nestled in the Sierra foothills near the town of Pollock Pines, just south of US Highway 50, the Sly Park Recreation Area is only about an hour from both South Lake Tahoe and Sacramento. Centered around the beautiful reservoir known as Jenkinson Lake, Sly Park has a variety of multi-use trails that are rideable nearly year round. The Jenkinson Lake Loop is an 8.8-mile route that circumnavigates the reservoir on the generally smooth and nontechnical mountain bike and hiking trail. The trail is well marked and has only 400 feet of climbing, making this a great ride for beginner and intermediate riders. This generally easy cruise does have the occasional technical rock garden to keep you on your toes and test your skills, but ever-present views of the lake make keeping your eyes on the trail a challenge.

GETTING THERE

From the Y intersection in South Lake Tahoe, travel south and then west on US Highway 50 for 43.6 miles; from Placerville, travel east on US 50 for 13.4 miles to Pollock Pines. Turn south onto Sly Park Road and follow it for 4.2 miles. Park near the entrance to the Sly Park Recreation Area, which charges a per-vehicle day-use fee. It also offers kayak and powerboat rentals and camping.

Mellow singletrack circumnavigates Sly Park Recreation Area's Jenkinson Lake.

MILEAGE LOG

0.0 Ride past the park gate and take a right turn toward the boat ramp and marina.

0.4 Pick up the trail at the south end of the marina parking area by the picnic tables.

0.9 Follow the trail up onto the road, watch for vehicles, and follow it east across the first dam.

1.2 Pick up the trail on the lake side of the road.

1.7 Ride across the second dam on the paved road.

1.8 Once past the dam, turn left again to pick up the trail on the lake side.

3.5 A number of more advanced secondary trails filter down to the lake trail in this area; they are typically accessed from higher up on Mormon Emigrant Trail.

4.5 Cross the bridge over Sly Park Creek. A short spur trail for hikers here leads to a waterfall.

5.3 Cross the bridge over Hazel Creek. From here, the route follows the road between campgrounds for a short distance.

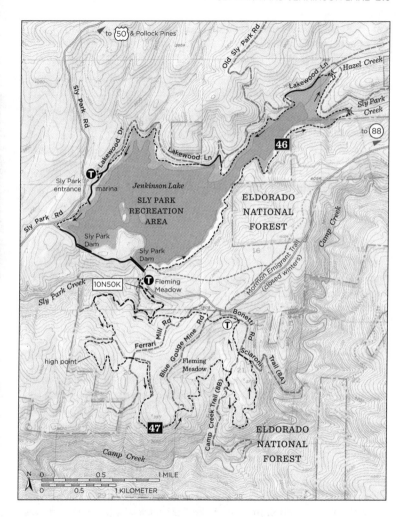

5.7 The trail drops to the left, off the road; keep your eyes peeled for this intersection.

7.1 Turn left back onto the paved road.

7.2 Turn left back onto the trail.

8.6   Arrive at the northern end of the marina. Turn right and head back up the hill to the park entrance.

8.8   Arrive at the parking area.

OPTIONS

You can ride this loop in either direction or, for a longer day, it is easily paired with Fleming Meadow (Route 47).

47 FLEMING MEADOW

LOOP

Trail Type: 80% singletrack, 20% doubletrack
Distance: 8 miles
Elevation Gain/Loss: 1200/1200 feet
High Point: 4070 feet
Ride Time: 45 minutes–2 hours

Technical Difficulty: Beginner
Fitness Intensity: Moderate
Season: Year-round
Map: USGS 7.5-minute, Sly Park
GPS: 38°42′50.32″ N, -120°33′37.90″ W

OVERVIEW

Adjacent to Jenkinson Lake and the Sly Park Recreation Area, the multi-use, nonmotorized Fleming Meadow recreation area has a great 8-mile loop known as Trail 8. The well-marked, rolling trail primarily features smooth, nontechnical singletrack that is significantly more exciting than the nearby trail around Jenkinson Lake. The trails in this area are at roughly 3500 feet in elevation and usually can be ridden year round.

GETTING THERE

From the Y intersection in South Lake Tahoe, travel south and then west on US Highway 50 for 43.6 miles; from Placerville, travel east on US 50 for 13.4 miles to Pollock Pines. Turn south onto Sly Park Road and follow it for 4.7 miles on Mormon Emigrant Trail, then follow it east across both dams of Jenkinson Lake for 0.8 mile and park in a dirt pullout on the south side of the road near Forest Road 10N50K.

MILEAGE LOG

0.0 Go around the locked Forest Service gate and head south on FR 10N50K.

0.6 At a right-hand bend in the road, Trail 8 comes in from the left. This is where you will finish the loop.

1.0 Doubletrack turns to singletrack.

1.6 After some steady climbing, cross a fire road.

2.0 Arrive at the top of the climb and the highest point of the ride, 4070 feet.

2.6 After a descent, the trail dumps you onto a doubletrack. Turn right and cross Ferrari Mill Rd. Just after crossing Ferrari Mill Rd., pick up the narrow singletrack on the right that parallels Blue Gouge Mine Rd.

3.0 Turn right, staying on singletrack on an old roadbed.

4.0 Stay straight on the singletrack.

4.9 Turn right on the doubletrack.

5.0 At the junction with the Camp Creek Trail (Trail 8B), stay on Trail 8 and continue on the fire road.

5.2 Turn left on the singletrack.

6.1 Pass the junction with the Sciaroni Trail (Trail 8A).

6.3 Continue straight on the singletrack that leads up to the alternate Fleming Meadow trailhead.

6.5 Stay left on the singletrack by the alternate trailhead parking area.

6.7 Cross Blue Gouge Mine Rd.

6.9 Cross Ferrari Mill Rd.

7.4 Turn right on the dirt road that you started on and head back toward the parking area.

8.0 Arrive at the parking area.

OPTIONS

At mile 5.0, a right turn on the Camp Creek Trail (Trail 8B) is a worthy diversion for those looking to add mileage or difficulty. This trail drops 0.8 mile steeply down into the Camp Creek drainage for a tough little out-and-back. You can also add mileage by turning right onto the Sciaroni Trail—a steep, old roadbed—at mile 6.1 for another 0.7 mile each way out-and-back ride. This loop is ideally situated to be combined with the Jenkinson Lake Loop to add mileage.

RENO AND CARSON CITY

As the two cities closest to Lake Tahoe, the Washoe Valley communities of Reno and Carson City, Nevada, are generally used for practicalities such as trips to the airport and less expensive groceries. More recently, however, people are making the trip down the hill to enjoy the ever-expanding and constantly improving trails the region has to offer. This is especially true in the spring, fall, and early winter when the trails around Reno and Carson City often remain snow free.

Situated just northeast of Lake Tahoe, Reno is known as the Biggest Little City in the World, but it isn't as little as it used to be. The Reno and Sparks metropolitan area is the second largest in the state, with an estimated population of nearly 450,000. Peavine Peak (Route 48) is the area's primary mountain biking destination, with an extensive and growing network of singletrack trails.

While it may be better known for the "bunny ranches" just outside of town, Carson City, the state capital, has a growing population of mountain bikers and a trail system that is growing in kind. The Ash Canyon to Kings Canyon Trail (Route 49) and the Clear Creek Trail (Route 50) are two fine examples of new trails in the area, with the Ash to Kings area so close that mountain bikers can ride to it right out of downtown. Carson City is also just a short distance from some of Tahoe's best riding on the east shore of the lake via US Highway 50.

Opposite: *Just west of Carson City, the Ash to Kings Trail is one of the newest additions to the area trail network.*

48 PEAVINE PEAK: KEYSTONE CANYON TO BACON STRIP

LOOP

Trail Type: 100% singletrack
Distance: 9.8 miles
Elevation Gain/Loss: 1550/1550 feet
High Point: 6360 feet
Ride Time: 1.5–3 hours

Technical Difficulty: Intermediate
Fitness Intensity: Moderate
Season: Early spring–late fall
Maps: USGS 7.5-minute, Reno, Verdi
GPS: 39°33'3.73" N, -119°50'56.4" W

OVERVIEW

Just northwest of Reno, Peavine Peak rises roughly 2500 vertical feet above the bright lights of downtown. Reno is known for its casinos, but this fair city is also home to fine mountain bike trails, and the lower flanks of Peavine Peak are covered in them. A vast network of fun singletrack crisscrosses this area, with virtually no limit on the ways these trails can be linked together. The trails and intersections are very well marked, so finding your way around is relatively easy.

Reno residents ride these trails all year while Tahoe riders frequent the area in the spring, fall, and winter months when the higher elevations are covered in snow. Be advised that there is little to no shade in this barren high desert landscape, and these trails can be inhospitable when it is extremely hot or windy.

Thanks largely to a group known as the Poedunks, the trail system continues to improve and expand. It is an excellent place to explore and to pick your favorite trails and loops, but the route described here features some of the best descents on the mountain.

The route begins with a gradual climb up Keystone Canyon before it ramps up on the Total Recall Trail and eventually finishes the ascent on the Scrub Brush Trail. Once atop the Bacon Strip you'll have great views of Reno and miles of fun singletrack descent below you. Join up with the Halo Trail and Poedunk Trail briefly before finishing the descent on the Fisticuffs Trail back down to Keystone Canyon.

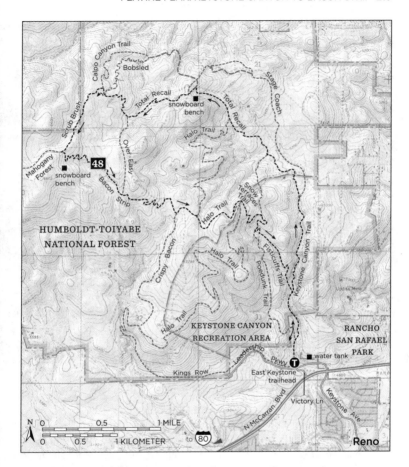

GETTING THERE

From US Highway 395, travel 3.3 miles west on North McCarran Boulevard, or from the junction of McCarran and Interstate 80, travel 2.2 miles north to Victory Lane. Turn north onto Victory Lane, then take the first right into the East Keystone trailhead. The parking area sits just west of a large and recognizable water tank on the hillside.

Peavine Peak's signature stark high desert landscape high above Reno

MILEAGE LOG

0.0 From the trailhead, head north into Keystone Canyon, following the trail that climbs gradually up through the bottom of the canyon. Numerous other trails intersect the canyon, but you want to stay on the Keystone Canyon Trail until you reach Total Recall.

1.4 Turn left onto Total Recall and begin to climb this narrow singletrack.

1.7 Pass through a gap in the fence then go straight across a dirt road; be sure to stay on the Total Recall Trail as it bears left.

2.1 Stay right at this junction with the Poedunk Trail to continue climbing on the Total Recall Trail.

2.7 Turn right at the junction with the Halo Trail and continue the climb on Total Recall.

3.2 As you crest the top of the climb, you'll spot one of the Peavine area's signature snowboard benches. The trail flattens out briefly before the final push to the top; stay on Total Recall.

3.9 Stay right past the junction with Over Easy and continue uphill on Total Recall.

4.3 Continue straight on Total Recall as Bobsled drops down on the right.

4.4 Continue uphill on Total Recall past the Calpo Canyon Trail.

4.5 At the top of Total Recall, ride straight across the dirt road and continue on Scrub Brush for the duration of the climb.

5.1 When Scrub Brush tops out at a junction with the Mahogany Forest and Bacon Strip trails, take a break and relax in the shade on the snowboard bench. From here, go left and begin the turn-filled descent of Bacon Strip. It crosses a dirt road almost immediately before the exciting descent begins.

6.9 Stay on Bacon Strip past the top of Crispy Bacon.

7.1 Merge onto the Halo Trail and follow it east.

7.7 After a few tight switchbacks, turn left off of Halo and onto the Snow Terraces Trail and continue descending. Stay on the Snow Terraces Trail until it merges with the Poedunk Trail; stay right and continue descending until you reach the Fisticuffs Trail.

8.4 Take a hard left onto the Fisticuffs Trail and continue descending.

9.1 The Fisticuffs Trail deposits you back down on the Keystone Canyon Trail. Take a right and coast back down toward the trailhead.

9.8 Arrive at the East Keystone trailhead.

OPTIONS

There is no limit to the ways you can connect and combine the trails of this network into loops of various lengths. There are so many trails and OHV roads that it can be a little dizzying to try and wrap your head around them all. If you are looking for more of a cross-country loop with a lot of up and down over its course, check out the Halo Trail by taking a left turn at mile 2.7 in the route described above. For another great downhill ride, try Bobsled. Take a right onto Bobsled at mile 4.3 and loop back to Total Recall via dirt roads to the lower snowboard bench. Another good option for your descent is to drop into Crispy Bacon at mile 6.9 and then follow the Halo Trail to pick up the route at mile 7.7. There are also several trails worthy of exploration just over the hill east of Keystone Canyon in Evans Canyon.

49 KINGS CANYON TO ASH CANYON

LOOP

Trail Type: 65% singletrack, 20% pavement, 15% doubletrack
Distance: 14.4 miles
Elevation Gain/Loss: 2200/2200 feet
High Point: 6743 feet
Ride Time: 1.5–3 hours

Technical Difficulty: Intermediate
Fitness Intensity: Strenuous
Season: Spring–late fall
Map: USGS 7.5-minute, Carson City
GPS: 39°10'44.14" N, -119°47'17.80" W

OVERVIEW

Created in a cooperative effort by the US Forest Service, Carson City, and a local group called Muscle Powered, the Kings Canyon to Ash Canyon Trail adds to the growing network in the area and makes for one of the best loops in the Washoe Valley. This incredibly scenic ride climbs, contours, and descends the steep hillsides directly above Carson City on a well-built, exciting singletrack. While this route can be done in either direction, a clockwise loop from Kings Canyon to Ash Canyon maximizes the downhill on singletrack. With the exception of the lower trails in Ash Canyon, the route is very well marked and easy to follow. This area can be incredibly hot in the midsummer months, so tackle it early or late in the day or during spring and fall when the weather is cooler and higher elevation trails are snowy.

Starting from the parking area on Foothill Drive, the route climbs for nearly 3 miles on pavement, which becomes a dirt road that leads you to the Kings Canyon trailhead. After joining the singletrack, you will climb gradually up to a beautiful waterfall before finishing the climbing on a short stretch of granny-gear-worthy dirt road. Once you get back on singletrack you will be on it down into Ash Canyon, then all the way back to the parking area.

GETTING THERE

From the intersection of North Carson Street (US Highway 395) and West Winnie Lane just north of downtown Carson City, head west on Winnie Lane

Climbing between Kings Canyon and Ash Canyon above Carson City

for 1.2 miles. Turn right onto Foothill Drive and park at the end of the street in the dirt parking area by the wooden fence.

MILEAGE LOG

0.0 Head back down Foothill Dr. for a few hundred feet and take a right onto West Winnie Ln.

0.3 Turn right onto Ash Canyon Rd.

0.6 Turn left onto Longview Way.

1.5 At the T-junction, turn right onto Kings Canyon Rd. and start the real climbing.

2.8 When the pavement ends, continue climbing on the dirt road. Stay on the main part of this road until you reach the Ash to Kings trailhead.

4.2 The singletrack begins when you see the trailhead kiosk and sign at a sharp switchback in the road. Enjoy the well-graded and generally pleasant singletrack as you climb up to the waterfall.

5.9 Cross over the waterfall on a bridge.

6.0 Turn hard left on the fire road, following the signs toward Ash Canyon, and begin the last of the climbing.

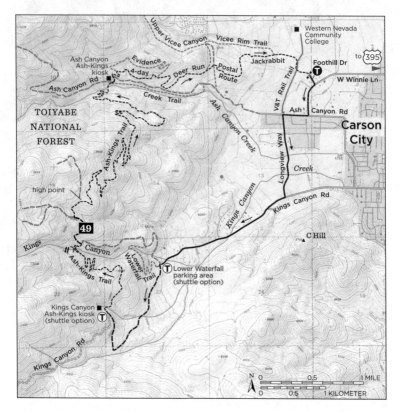

6.6 Turn right, back onto the singletrack, at the top of this dirt road climb. This intersection is well marked with signs. From here it is almost entirely downhill to the parking area, and there are amazing views the entire way. Be on the lookout for some very sharp switchbacks as there are quite a few throughout this descent.

11.5 The Ash to Kings Trail ends at the trailhead on Ash Canyon Rd. There are various ways down from here, including the road, but you can ride sweet singletrack all the way back to the car, so why wouldn't you? Take a right on Ash Canyon Rd.

11.6 Take the first trail you see on the left and climb up it for just a few hundred feet.

11.7 Take a right. This singletrack goes all the way to the parking area. As you descend, stay on the main trail and continue downhill at any intersections.

14.2 Ride straight across the paved V&T Rail Trail and follow the singletrack around the hole in the ground, behind the houses, and to the end of Foothill Dr.

14.4 Arrive at the parking area on Foothill Dr.

OPTIONS

You can shuttle to avoid riding the pavement by parking at the Lower Waterfall Trail parking area. Or to avoid both the pavement and the dirt road, park at the Kings Canyon Ash to Kings kiosk to save a few miles of climbing at the beginning of this route.

50 CLEAR CREEK TRAIL

OUT-AND-BACK

Trail Type: 92% singletrack, 8% pavement
Distance: 19.4 miles
Elevation Gain/Loss: 2080/2080 feet
High Point: 6171 feet
Ride Time: 2–4 hours

Technical Difficulty: Intermediate
Fitness Intensity: Moderate
Season: Spring–late fall (sometimes year-round)
Map: USGS 7.5-minute, Genoa
GPS: 39°5'30.53" N, -119°48'20.93" W

OVERVIEW

One of the best rides in the Carson City area, the recently completed and nearly all-singletrack Clear Creek Trail takes riders on a circuitous route from the sagebrush desert of the Carson Valley up to the pine forests of the lower western slope of the Carson Range and features incredible views along its entire length.

On the ride, you'll make a gradual and relatively consistent climb before a short descent to the turnaround point at the top of the trail. The trail has both sandy and dirt surfaces, and the lower portion may occasionally be quite

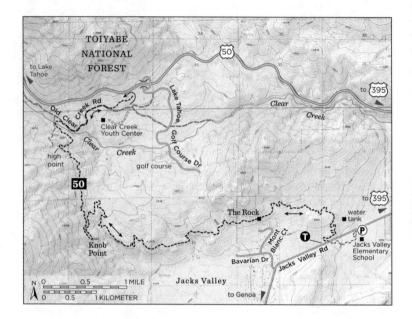

loose. It crosses numerous dirt roads but is incredibly well marked and easy to follow. Please respect the various private landowners by staying on the designated trail. Since there is currently no access to this trail from the top, it is ridden only as an out-and-back from Jacks Valley Road. This trail's low elevation also lends itself well to being rideable very early and very late in the season, with the potential for midwinter riding, depending on snow levels. All in all, this well-built multiuse trail is a fabulous addition to the Carson Valley's growing trail network.

GETTING THERE

From the southern junction of US Highway 50 and South Carson Street (US Highway 395) in Carson City, head 1.8 miles south on US 395. Turn west on Jacks Valley Road and continue for 1.5 miles to a large dirt parking area on the right (north) side of the road by a trailhead kiosk. There is additional parking in a large lot next to the Jacks Valley Elementary School, which is on the south side of the road, 0.5 mile east of the trailhead. There's

Heading up the Cold Creek Trail above Jacks Valley Road and Carson Valley

a trail that runs on the south side of Jacks Valley Road from the school to the trailhead.

MILEAGE LOG

0.0 From the parking area on the north side of Jacks Valley Rd., head north through the fence and begin the gradual ascent through sandy soil and sagebrush. Follow the signs as the trail makes several turns in the first quarter mile or so.

2.2 There is a brief respite in the climbing after you pass through a rocky saddle known as "The Rock" above the homes on Mont Blanc Ct. The trail soon enters the forest, offering shade.

3.5 Begin the long, gradual climb up to Knob Point.

6.3 At Knob Point, the trail flattens out briefly before climbing again up to the trail's high point.

7.8 Arrive at the ride's high point at 6171 feet.

8.3 Join a dirt road very briefly, crossing the creek, then take a right back onto the singletrack.

8.5 Merge onto the pavement of the Old Clear Creek Road and descend. This road is a mix of old broken pavement and dirt and is closed to vehicles.

9.2 Turn left back onto singletrack; this junction is marked with a sign.

9.7 Turn around at the end of the trail.

10.2 Turn right back onto Old Clear Creek Road and begin climbing.

10.9 Turn left back onto the singletrack; this intersection is marked with a sign.

11.1 Turn left when the trail intersects a doubletrack, cross the creek, and stay left back onto the singletrack.

11.6 Arrive back at the trail's high point; it's almost entirely downhill from here.

13.1 Pass by Knob Point.

17.2 Pass by the Rock again and begin the last part of the descent. The trail is twisty and turn-filled; be aware that the sand may be loose if it hasn't rained in a while.

19.4 Arrive at the parking area.

OPTIONS

Feel free to turn around on this out-and-back ride when you prefer. Most people turn around when they reach Old Clear Creek Road. There are plans to connect the top of this trail to the Ash-Kings Canyon trail network, so stay tuned.

APPENDIX:
BIKE PARKS

In addition to the hundreds of miles of excellent singletrack trails in the Tahoe region, a number of bike parks now add to the already long list of amazing riding opportunities. Truckee's Northstar offers the area's only lift-served downhill mountain biking park and limitless gravity-fed excitement. Two new community supported bike parks, the Truckee Bike Park and South Lake Tahoe's Bijou Bike Park, both provide a free-to-all, unique riding experience. The Truckee and Bijou bike parks both offer something for all ages and ability levels with pump tracks, flow lines, dirt jumps, and learning and progression zones. They provide an environment where everyone from kids on strider bikes to local pros can have a great time learning, practicing, and progressing in their skills.

Bijou Bike Park
Bijou Community Park
1301 Al Tahoe Blvd.
South Lake Tahoe, CA 96150
www.bijoubikepark.org

South Lake Tahoe's Bijou Bike Park officially opened on September 19, 2015. Thanks to the hard work of the City of South Lake Tahoe, the Tahoe Area Mountain Biking Association (TAMBA), and South Lake Tahoe BMX, this dream has become a reality, and area residents now have brand-new, large and small pump tracks, a BMX track, three slopestyle lines, and a loop trail to choose from. This world-class facility is the first of its kind within the Tahoe basin and is designed to accommodate riders of all abilities, from small children to seasoned pros.

Incline Bike Project
Incline Village, NV

A bike park project is in the works that would include a pump track and skills areas in the town of Incline Village, Nevada. As of the time this book went to press, this project was still in the planning stages but could come to fruition in the next few years.

Northstar
5001 Northstar Dr.
Truckee, CA 96161
www.northstarcalifornia.com

Northstar offers a variety of mountain biking services, including an extensive network of lift-serviced downhill trails, cross-country trails, bike rentals, sales, and lessons. Be sure to check their website for current days and hours of operation, ticket pricing, and special events.

Truckee Bike Park
12304 Joerger Dr.
Truckee, CA 96161
www.truckeebikepark.org

One of Truckee's most exciting new mountain biking options, the non-profit, volunteer supported, privately funded Truckee Bike Park is free for all to enjoy and has been steadily growing over the past several years. The park now features a pump track, dirt jumps, a dual slalom course, flow lines, a drop zone, and a short (half-mile) cross-country loop. There is something for riders of all abilities here, with the goal of facilitating learning, practicing skills, and having fun.

RESOURCES

TRAIL MAINTENANCE AND ADVOCACY

Bicyclists of Nevada County
Nevada City, CA
www.bonc.org

Folsom Auburn Trail Riders Action Coalition (FATRAC)
Auburn, CA
www.fatrac.org

Muscle Powered
Carson City, NV
www.musclepowered.org

Poedunks
Reno, NV
www.poedunk.org

Sierra Buttes Trail Stewardship
Clio, CA
www.sierratrails.org

Tahoe Area Mountain Biking Association (TAMBA)
South Lake Tahoe, CA
www.tamba.org

Tahoe Rim Trail Association (TRTA)
Stateline, NV
www.tahoerimtrail.org

Truckee Donner Land Trust
Truckee, CA
ww.tdlandtrust.org

Truckee Trails Foundation
Truckee, CA
www.truckeetrails.org

SHUTTLE SERVICES

Downieville Outfitters
114 Main Street
Downieville, CA 95936
(530) 289-0155
www.downievilleoutfitters.com

Flume Trail Mountain Bikes
1115 Tunnel Creek Road
Incline Village, NV 89451
(775) 298-2501
www.flumetrailtahoe.com

Over the Edge
3665 Tamarack Avenue
South Lake Tahoe, CA 96150
(530) 600-3633
www.otesports.com/locations/south
-lake-tahoe

Wanna Ride Tahoe Shuttle
(775) 790-6375
www.wannaridetahoe.com

Yuba Expeditions
208 Main Street
Downieville, CA 95936
(530) 289-3010
www.yubaexpeditions.com

GUIDE SERVICES

Tahoe Adventure Company
7010 North Lake Boulevard
Tahoe Vista, CA 96148
(530) 913-9212
www.tahoeadventurecompany.com

Tahoe Mountain Guides
10095 West River Street
Truckee, CA 96161
(530) 686-5895
www.tahoemountainguides.com

BIKE SHOPS

North Lake Tahoe

Factory Bike
3039 Highway 89
Olympic Valley, CA 96146
(530) 581-3399
www.squawbikes.com

Gravity Shop
475 North Lake Boulevard
Tahoe City, CA 96145
(530) 581-2558
www.tahoegravityshop.com

Olympic Bike Shop
620 North Lake Boulevard
Tahoe City, CA 96145
(530) 581-2500
www.olympicbikeshop.com

Village Ski Loft
800 Tahoe Boulevard
Incline Village, NV 89451
(775) 831-3537
www.villageskiloft.com

West Shore Sports
5395 West Lake Boulevard
Homewood, CA 96141
(530) 525-9920
www.westshoresports.com

Truckee

The Backcountry
11400 Donner Pass Road, # 100
Truckee, CA 96161
(530) 582-0909
www.thebackcountry.net

Cyclepaths
10095 West River Street
Truckee, CA 96161
(530) 582-1890
www.cyclepaths.com

Paco's Bike and Ski
12047 Donner Pass Road
Truckee, CA 96161
(530) 587-5561
www.pacosxc.com

Start Haus
10990 Donner Pass Road
Truckee, CA 96161
(530) 582-5781
www.starthaus.com

Tahoe Donner Bike Works
15275 Alder Creek Road
Truckee, CA 96161
(530) 582-9694
www.tahoedonner.com

South Lake Tahoe

Over the Edge
3665 Tamarack Avenue
South Lake Tahoe, CA 96150
(530) 600-3633
www.otesports.com/locations/south
-lake-tahoe/

Sierra Ski and Cycle Works
3430 Lake Tahoe Boulevard
South Lake Tahoe, CA 96150
(530) 541-7505
www.sierraskiandcycleworks.com

South Shore Bikes
871 Emerald Bay Road
South Lake Tahoe, CA 96150
(530) 544-7433
http://bikes.southshorebikeand
snow.com/

Tahoe Sports Ltd.
4000 Lake Tahoe Boulevard, #7
South Lake Tahoe, CA 96150
(530) 542-4000
www.tahoesportsltd.com

Watta Bike Shop
2933 Highway 50
Meyers, CA 96150
(530) 544-7700
www.wattabike.com

LAND MANAGERS

US Forest Service

Eldorado National Forest
100 Forni Road
Placerville, CA 95667
(530) 622-5061
www.fs.usda.gov/eldorado/

   Pacific Ranger District
   7887 Highway 50
   Pollock Pines, CA 95726
   (530) 644-2349

   Placerville Ranger District
   4260 Eight Mile Road
   Camino, CA 95709
   (530) 644-2324

Humboldt-Toiyabe National Forest
1200 Franklin Way
Sparks, NV 89431
(775) 331-6444
www.fs.usda.gov/htnf

   Carson Ranger District
   1536 South Carson Street
   Carson City, NV 89701
   (775) 882-2766

Lake Tahoe Basin Management Unit
35 College Drive
South Lake Tahoe, CA 96150
(530) 543-2600
www.fs.usda.gov/ltbmu

Plumas National Forest
159 Lawrence Street
Quincy, CA 95971
(530) 283-2050
www.fs.usda.gov/plumas

   Beckwourth Ranger District
   23 Mohawk Road
   PO Box 7
   Blairsden, CA 96103
   (530) 836-2575

Tahoe National Forest
631 Coyote Street
Nevada City, CA 95959
(530) 265-4531
www.fs.usda.gov/tahoe

   American River Ranger District
   22830 Foresthill Road
   Foresthill, CA 95631
   (530) 367-2224

   Sierraville Ranger District
   317 South Lincoln Street
   PO Box 95
   Sierraville, CA 96126
   (530) 994-3401

Truckee Ranger District
10811 Stockrest Springs Road
Truckee, CA 96161
(530) 587-3558

STATE PARKS

California

Burton Creek State Park
Northeast of Tahoe City, CA 96145
(530) 525-7232
www.parks.ca.gov/?page_id=512

Ed Z'berg Sugar Pine Point State Park
7360 West Lake Boulevard
Tahoma, CA 96142
(530) 525-7982
www.parks.ca.gov/?page_id=510

Nevada

Main Office:
901 South Stewart Street
5th Floor, Suite 5005
Carson City, NV 89701
(775) 684-2770

Lake Tahoe Nevada State Park, Spooner Backcountry
PO Box 6116
Incline Village, NV 89452
(775) 831-0494
http://parks.nv.gov/parks/marlette-hobart-backcountry/

Van Sickle Bi-State Park
PO Box 6116
Incline Village, NV 89452
(775) 831-0494
http://parks.nv.gov/parks/van-sickle/

Other Parks

Sly Park Recreation Area
4771 Sly Park Road
Pollock Pines, CA 95726
(530) 295-6824

INDEX

A

Animal Crackers, 175–178
Animal Trail, 175–178
Andesite Ridge and Peak,
  164–167, 171
Angora Ridge Trail, 153–155
Antone Meadows, 47–51, 54
Armstrong
  Connector, 127, 132,
    143–144
  Pass, 124–128, 132–138,
    145
  Pass Trail, 124–127,
    132–134, 136–138, 144
Ash Canyon, 217, 222–225
Ash Canyon to Kings Can-
  yon Trail, 217, 222–225
Auburn, CA, 201, 207–209

B

Backcountry, The, 232
Bacon Strip, 218–221
Baldy, Mount, 75, 78–82, 85
Bench, The, 105–108,
  110–111
Bicyclists of Nevada County,
  14, 202, 231
Big Boulder, 194–195
Big Meadow, 131, 135–139,
  146–148
Boca Hill, 182
Brockway Summit, 43,
  71–75, 79–84
Burton Creek State Park,
  46–48, 234
Butcher Ranch, 190–195

C

Carson City, NV, 107, 217,
  222–226
Castle Peak, 164–171
Chimney Beach Trail, 91–95,
  102–104
Christmas Valley Trail,
  145–148
Clear Creek Trail, 217,
  225–228
Cold Creek Trail, 116,
  118–127, 135, 140–142
Confluence Trail, 201, 210
Connector Trail, 209, 210
Corral Trails, 13, 115–116,
  128, 132, 135, 141–145
Culvert Trail, 201, 210
Cyclepaths, 232

D

Daggett Pass, 131
Deveron Connector, 155
Diamond Peak, 88–90, 93,
  97, 100
Donner Lake Rim Trail, 161,
  167–171, 175
Donner Summit, 161, 164,
  168–171
Downieville, CA, 189–195
Downieville Outfitters, 231
Drifter Hut, 168–171

E

Ed Z'berg Sugar Pine Point
  State Park, 234

Eldorado National Forest,
  233
Emigrant Trail, 175, 178–181
Euer Valley, 172–175

F

Factory Bike, 232
Fiberboard Freeway, 43–58,
  63–64, 67–73
First Divide, 191–195
Fisticuffs, 218–221
Fleming Meadow, 201,
  214–215
Flume Trail, 87, 95–96,
  99–104
Flume Trail Mountain
  Bikes, 231
Foresthill Divide Trail, 201,
  207–210
Fountain Place Road,
  124–127, 132–134, 142–145
Freel Pass, 124–128,
  135–138
Fuel Break Trail, 209–210

G

General Creek Trail,
  156–159
Genoa, NV, 108–113
Glass Mountain, 43–46,
  72, 75
Gold Lake Highway, 189,
  193, 198–199
Graeagle, CA, 189, 198
Gravity Shop, 232
Gun Mount, 149–152

H

Halo Trail, 218–221
Hawley Grade, 148
High Meadows, 116–127
Hole in the Ground, 164–168
Humboldt-Toiyabe National Forest, 233

I

Incline Flume, 89–90, 100
Incline Village, NV, 87, 88, 91, 96, 103
International Mountain Bicycling Association (IMBA), 20–21

J

Jackass Ridge, 162–163
Jenkinson Lake, 201, 211, 213

K

Keystone Canyon, 218–221
Kings Canyon, 217, 222–225
Kingsbury Grade, 105, 108–111, 119, 131, 137, 139
Kings Beach, CA, 31, 72, 79, 82–85
Kings Beach Trails, 82–85

L

Lake Tahoe
    altitude, 16
    climate, 14–16
    flora and fauna, 16–17
Lake Tahoe Basin Management Unit, 15, 233
Lake Tahoe Nevada State Park, Spooner Backcountry, 234
Lloyds, 181–183
Lost Lake, 158–159
Luther Pass, 115, 132–135, 137

M

Marlette Lake, 93–96, 99–100, 103–104
Marlette Peak, 87, 93–96, 99–100
Martis Peak, 79–85
Meyers, CA, 115, 132, 135, 143, 146
Mills Peak, 189, 195–199
Missing Link, 59–62
Monument Pass, 115–120, 131, 137, 139
Mount Baldy, 78–82, 85
Mount Watson, 55–57, 59, 62–67
Mr. Toad's Wild Ride, 131–135, 137

N

Negro Canyon, 168–171
Nevada City, CA, 201–207
Nordic Center (Tahoe XC), 47–55, 63–67
North Canyon Rd, 103–104

O

Old Mount Rose Highway, 88–89
Olympic Bike Shop, 232
OTB (Over the Bars), 67–71
Over the Edge, 231, 232

P

Packer Saddle, 189–194
Paco's Bike and Ski, 232
Page Meadows, 31–38
Painted Rock, 51–54, 67–68, 72, 75
Pauley Creek, 193–195
Peavine Peak, 217–221
Pioneer Trail, 201–207
Plumas National Forest, 233
Poedunk Trail, 218–221
Pollock Pines, CA, 201, 211, 213

Powerline Trail
    North Lake, 46, 75
    South Lake, 116, 119–120, 139–143, 145
Prosser
    Creek, 178, 181–182
    Dam, 181–184
    Hill, 175–178

R

Railroad Grade, 125, 127, 142
Red House Flume, 96, 99
Reno, NV, 217, 218
Reservoir Trail, 47–50
Rusty's, 32–34, 37–38

S

Saddle Road Connector, 118–120, 131
Sawtooth Ridge, 184–187
Scotts Flat Trail, 201–204
Scott Peak, 35–38
Scrub Brush, 218–221
Second Divide, 191–195
Sidewinder Trail
    South Lake, 144–145
    Tahoe Donner, 174–175
Sierra Buttes Trail Stewardship, 11, 14, 190, 195, 231
Sierra Canyon, 108–113
Sierra Ski and Cycle Works, 233
Sly Park Recreation Area, 201, 211–214, 234
Snapdragon Trail, 87, 96–99
South Camp Peak, 107, 111
South Lake Tahoe, CA, 115–155
South Shore Bikes, 233
Spooner Backcountry, 234
Spooner Lake, 96, 102–104
Spooner Summit, 105–111
Squaw Valley Downhill, 76–77

Stagecoach Trailhead,
128–129, 131, 136–139
Stampede Reservoir,
178–181
Stanford Rock, 39–42
Star Lake Trail, 115–116,
118–127, 137, 139
Start Haus, 232
Stateline, NV, 115, 128–129
Stump Meadows, 43–45
Sugar Pine Point State Park
(Ed Z'berg), 156–159
Summit Lake, 168–171
Sunflower Hill Trail, 87, 94,
96, 99
Sunrise Trail and Sunrise
Flow Trail, 190, 192–195

T
Tahoe Adventure Company,
232
Tahoe Area Mountain Bik-
ing Association (TAMBA),
11, 13, 96, 115, 231
Tahoe City, CA, 31–59
Tahoe Donner, 161, 168–175
Tahoe Donner Bike Works,
232
Tahoe Mountain, 115–116,
149–156

Tahoe Mountain Guides,
232
Tahoe National Forest, 233
Tahoe Rim Trail, 12, 31–146
(throughout book)
Tahoe Rim Trail Associa-
tion, 11–13, 231
Tahoe XC (Nordic Center),
47–55, 63–67
Tahoma, CA, 156–158
Tahoe Sports Ltd., 233
Third Divide, 191–194
Total Recall, 218–221
Truckee, CA, 161–187
Truckee Trails Foundation,
13, 231
Tunnel Creek
Road, 91, 95–96, 99–100,
103
Station, 95–96, 100,
103–104
Twin Peaks, 41–43
Tyrolean Downhill, 87–100

U
US Forest Service Lake
Tahoe Basin Management
Unit, 13, 115

V
Van Sickle Trail, 115–116,
119–120, 128–131, 139
Van Sickle Bi-State Park,
128–131, 139
Village Ski Loft, 232

W
Wall, the, 59–62, 68–71
Wall-ternate, 59–62, 68, 71
Wanna Ride Tahoe Shuttle,
231
Ward Creek, 39–43
Watson Lake, 55–59, 63–67,
72–74
Watson, Mount, 55–57, 59,
62–67
Watta Bike Shop, 233
Western States Trail, 59–61,
68, 71, 76–77
West Shore Sports, 232
Whoop-de-doo Trail, 47–55,
58, 63–64

Y
Yuba Expeditions, 232

ABOUT THE AUTHOR

Heather Benson

Jeremy Benson has been living and mountain biking in the Lake Tahoe area since 2001. A New England native, Benson moved to Tahoe after graduating from Saint Michael's College in Vermont to ski for a year before getting a "real job." All these years later, he's still skiing and mountain biking to his heart's content in the year-round playground that is Lake Tahoe. A longtime sponsored ski athlete, Benson is also the author of the forthcoming *Backcountry Ski & Snowboard Routes: California* (Mountaineers Books). In addition to freelance writing, Benson supports his lifestyle as a waiter in a fine dining restaurant in Tahoe City. He currently resides in Truckee, California, with his wife, Heather. Depending on the season, you can find him on the singletrack or the skin track enjoying the mountains and life to the fullest.